# Sean Gresh

# BECOMING
# A FATHER

## A Handbook for
## Expectant Fathers

## Butterick Publishing

*Design by Joan Croom*

**Library of Congress Cataloging in Publication Data**

**Gresh, Sean.**
  **Becoming a father.**

Bibliography: p. 140
Includes index.
1. Pregnancy.  2. Childbirth.  3. Infants (Newborn)—Care and hygiene.  4. Fathers.  I. Title.
RG525.G74      649'.1'0242      80-19399
ISBN 0-88421-099-5

Manufactured and printed in the United States of America, published simultaneously in the USA and Canada.

# Contents

# Foreword

The father's participation in childbearing is a very recent development. The mother-infant dyad has become a mother-father-infant triad.

The customs and cultural patterns leading up to this development have varied greatly in the last three centuries. Generally, in the eighteenth century childbirth was regarded as a merry time, at least for the father, where festivities should take place. In Scotland, for example, a special drink called "groaning malt" was offered with a rich cheese cake while a wife was giving birth. In England, men held "confinement parties."

In the nineteenth century the picture changed. Husbands did not arrange parties during childbirth and their responses were much less romantic than they had been a century earlier. Men found the time of pregnancy, labor, and delivery particularly worrisome. A very real fear they held was of their wives dying during childbirth, and one of their special concerns was often financial. For the most part, families were large and, as a character in a novel of the period noted, "children are expensive things."

In the first half of the twentieth century the customs changed yet again and fathers were separated entirely from their laboring wives. But this separation was hard for a husband to face, especially since it often troubled him that giving birth was so painful and difficult.

By the middle of the twentieth century a woman was even more isolated than when she had given birth in her own home. Not only was she separated from her husband and her familiar surroundings, but she was put in a sterile, cell-like room in a hospital. She was left alone, frightened. The whole process of childbirth seemed to have become removed from all emotions and feelings and was entirely oriented toward strict medical surroundings where the fetus or the baby was much more important than the mother's welfare and feelings. The father was detached from the process. He was allowed to pay the bills and keep out of the way, and was only called in when his wife had given birth. It seems strange, but he was well supported by the current cultural thought that being mixed up with childbirth was not something that enhanced a man's image. It was a woman's job, not anything in which a man should be closely involved.

However, in the second half of the twentieth century, the father's role during his wife's labor and delivery has slowly become one of active participation. It is almost as if the customs and experiences of three centuries have been thrown together, albeit in a humane and constructive way. Joyous parties have been introduced again by celebrating the birth of the baby with a bottle of champagne—sometimes right in the hospital. The anxieties that were so dominant in the nineteenth century are actually still with us: Fathers still worry a great deal about their financial responsibilities, but with the knowledge that they do not have to have a large family.

*Becoming a Father* shows a wonderful understanding of the changed role of the father in our present society. Sean Gresh quite obviously speaks from his own experience. He is a modern father whose great humanity and warmth show up in every chapter. It is reassuring to read his words on sex and pregnancy; to read what many fathers and mothers felt during their pregnancies and deliveries; to be able to identify and realize that none of us has to be alone and lost in our anxieties and joys. The "choosing and planning," as the author calls it, will help every new and expectant father, and I would like to think that this book will reassure them all, nervous or not so nervous, and make them feel more confident to take up their new roles as active partners in the birth and parenting of their children.

Elisabeth Bing
Clinical Assistant Professor
Department of Obstetrics and Gynecology
New York Medical College

# Acknowledgments

The idea for writing *Becoming a Father* originated five years ago when my wife, Kathy Hoffman, was pregnant with our first child, Kristen, and we were living in Waterville, a picturesque village nestled in the mountains of northern Vermont. In the course of researching the book and actually experiencing the changes and challenges of becoming a father, I have talked to and interviewed expectant fathers and mothers, new parents, researchers, childbirth educators, obstetricians, pediatricians, psychologists, psychiatrists, nurses, hospital administrators, and many, many others in all parts of this country and in Canada. I wish to thank all of these persons for their generous cooperation and support.

First and foremost, I wish to thank my wife Kathy for her loving support, her patience, and her sense of humor. Her support enabled me to keep a sense of balance about *Becoming a Father,* the book project, and about the reality of actually becoming a father. Kathy has helped me to understand better that to become a father literally means a total sharing with the mother of one's children in the joys and responsibilities of being an active parent, regardless of whether one plays a traditional or a nontraditional role.

The following is a partial list of those whom I wish to thank for their cooperation and assistance: Elisabeth Bing, Rona Cherry, Josanne Wilson, Ross Parke, Charles E. Gresh, Michael Yogman, Robert Carr, Libby Colman, Lois Wandersman, James Hahn, Joel Sussman, Philip Levin, Robert Fein, Linda Lefton, George Rentz, Tommy Lloyd, Carolyn Cowan, Philip Cowan, Anita Tamari, Lynn Cheney, and all the men who generously talked to me about every aspect of their experiences in becoming fathers.

I wish also to acknowledge the valuable contributions made by my editor, Linnea Leedham, and my literary agent, Denise Marcil.

Writing *Becoming a Father* represents only one part of a complex process involving lots of people, some of whom I have just acknowledged. But two other groups of people involved in this process often go unacknowledged. One group consists of those who physically produce, promote, distribute, and sell the book, and to all these persons I express my appreciation and respect. The other group are those who buy and read *Becoming a Father* and respond to what they read. To these persons—to you—I express my appreciation and, most important, my hope that you consider *Becoming a Father* part of a dialogue. I invite you, therefore, to respond to the ideas discussed in *Becoming a Father* by writing to me about your experiences and observations about becoming a father. Your response will be enormously helpful to me as I continue researching and writing about men and the experiences they and their wives have as they become new parents. You can write to me in care of Butterick Publishing or at P. O. Box 14, Bradford, Massachusetts 01830.

For Kathy, Kristen, and Geoffrey,
and for my father, Charles F. Gresh.

# 1

# To Be a Father

In the early decades of the twentieth century, a father was considered something akin to a benevolent ruler, a boss of sorts, who was primarily an authoritarian figure; but in the late 1940s and 1950s, his role became unclear. Television and the movies, two barometers that reflect general changes in the culture, often portrayed father as a good-natured but confused and bumbling figure, whose main responsibilities were to earn money and to stay out of the kitchen. With the current attention being given fathers, their position has improved, but it is still a tenuous one.

"Human fatherhood is a social invention," wrote the late anthropologist Margaret Mead. "Men have to learn to want to provide for others, and this behavior, being learned, is rather fragile and can disappear rather easily under social conditions that no longer teach it effectively."

Until recently, social attitudes have not been strongly supportive of fathers who wanted to play an active role at the birth of their children. Speaking of an expectant father's situation, childbirth educator and author Elisabeth Bing said, "An expectant father should have a strong role as a coach, as a participant. After all, it's his child, too. He's needed to give all the strength and support and empathy he can, but he has to be encouraged to do so, because in our culture he's not strongly supported to play an active role. He's still the odd man out."

## Options for Fathers

Thanks to the work of Elisabeth Bing, thousands of others in the childbirth education movement, and hundreds of thousands of fathers who have attended and participated in the birth of their children, the attitudes toward fathering have gone through dramatic changes. Books on fathering are plentiful as are movies, novels, and television programs that feature stories of fathers. This focus on fathers reflects a strong, nationwide movement of men who are becoming more active parents—taking on more responsibility, doing more with their children right from the start, and enjoying their newly appreciated status as fathers. Also contributing to the improved climate has been a recent dramatic increase in research about fathers.

With all the attention fathers are getting there is the danger that the movement toward more involved fathers will wind up pressuring men into doing things they are uncomfortable doing because these are the "in" things to do. The herd mentality is antithetical to what those who study fathers would like to see happen. "I am concerned," said Dr. Robert Fein, a Harvard University psychologist who conducted a major study of expectant fathers, "with the pressure placed on a father that the only way for his wife to have a baby is for him to be there with her. One expectant father I know, who is a supermasculine type—he's a construction worker, in fact—said 'Yuk, I wouldn't have anything to do with that stuff. I'll never go in there with my wife. But if she wants it, I'll do it.' When I saw him after the birth," continued Fein, "he told me, 'I've been telling all the guys, the only way to be a real man is to be there at the birth. It was a great experience.' " Dr. Fein believes fathers should have choices. "I felt uncomfortable about his attitude. This is something fathers ought to have the opportunity to do if they want to. If they don't, that's okay. If they do, it's okay. But it's a decision that a husband and his wife have to make together."

Dr. Fein and other researchers studying fathers feel strongly that there are many ways of being a father. The research they are doing and the popular acceptance it has received bolster their position that in the improved social climate fathers have more options. They can play the role of traditional fathers and still share more of the responsibilities of child care evenings and weekends; or they can create new roles for themselves ranging from staying at home full-time with their children while their wives work to sharing child care on a 50–50 basis.

Dr. Michael Yogman, a pediatrician at Harvard University's Medical School, has been conducting several major studies of how fathers interact with infants. He is also concerned about the pressure on fathers to do the latest or "right" thing as fathers. Said Dr. Yogman, "There is so much of a premium put on doing the right thing with your baby that people become very insecure about it. It makes them feel that if the slightest thing goes wrong, for example, if the baby fusses or frowns, then they haven't done the right thing. Fathers in particular are very vulnerable and very sensitive to this insecurity. Fathers should feel comfortable with how they act as fathers. This is more important than trying to conform to how some psychologist or pediatrician says they should act. The real goal of this research is not to tell people how to act, but to increase the range of options available to them."

## Why Become a Father?

With contemporary contraception and family planning, becoming a father often is a matter of choice, not of chance. But why become a father? In a recent article in a popular magazine for parents,* the author listed and discussed the right and wrong reasons for having another child. While such discussions may be helpful, more than reason is involved. "Why a person has a child," said Dr. Robert Carr, a Toronto child psychiatrist, "has to do with very primary, instinctual material, and so it often defies reason. If you had any sense, you wouldn't have children—it's crazy." A father of two young boys himself, Dr. Carr is quick to point out that it's crazy only if you look at having children at a practical level. At this level, the time and energy—not to mention the costs—of having a child are considerations you must look at carefully. But above all else, your deepest feelings must be your ultimate guide. If these feelings are mostly positive, you are off to a good start.

*Leah Yarrow, "Right and Wrong Reasons for Having Another Baby," **Parents Magazine,** January 1979, pages 45–47.

Remember, of course, that it takes two to get pregnant and that both you and your wife have to feel that having a child is, deep down, what you want to do and what you believe you should do. Even though you feel in your bones that having a child is right for you, don't be surprised if your conviction is accompanied by doubts and worries: Will I be a good father? Is it the right thing to do? Am I ready? It is natural to believe deeply in something and at the same time have many doubts and concerns. The most important thing, according to Dr. Carr, is to follow your deepest instincts: "I think it should be acknowledged that the majority of people can make good parents and that they should have confidence in themselves."

Trusting your feelings and following your instincts is not as easy as it sounds. But it's not all that difficult, either. Being an expectant father is a process. "When you talk about becoming a father or being an expectant father," said childbirth educator Linda Lefton, "you're really talking about the experience of the evolution of a father." You can make a more successful transition to becoming a father if you keep in mind that you can be a good father and that it is a matter of *being* and not *doing*. No one can tell you how to be a father. Being a father cannot be reduced to a series of actions or a list of rules. "How-to" books on parenting or being a father, therefore, are inappropriate in that they assume that the purpose of being a father is to come up with an end product—a perfectly developed human being—much as an automobile manufacturer produces cars. On the contrary, what you are becoming is a father and that is a state of being—of being someone, of being in relation to another, of being toward another. Being a father is a role defined by the relationship to one's child or children. Ultimately, it has to do with loving. In a column about being a father,* Garry Wills wrote, "Loving is not simply doing or being done to—it is a way of being *toward* another, an unceasing transactional 'being-with.' " Trusting your own instincts and feelings, therefore, means everything.

## What's It Like?

The climate is better. The choice is yours (with your wife). There are many options available regarding roles. But what is it really like to become a father? What about all the changes one has to make, all the inconvenience? Walter Abrams of Lexington, Massachusetts, and the father of a young daughter, presents an example of what most fathers experience. "People who don't have children," said Walter, "worry so much about changes in their lifestyle. I know I did. But these changes are so trivial compared to the gains. It's impossible beforehand to know what it's going to be like—the positive stuff in particular. You can imagine what it's like to have a screaming child who prevents you from doing something, but you can't imagine what it feels like, what that love feels like, until you become a father. It's wonderful."

*Garry Wills, "On Being a Parent," **Parents Magazine,** January 1979, page 115.

# 2

# What's Ahead for Expectant Fathers

Tim and Sheryl had been married for five years. They met at the University of Georgia, fell in love, and married after graduation. When Sheryl was in her late twenties, she became anxious about waiting much longer to have their first child. She and Tim wanted a child, but the responsibility of raising one worried them. They also worried about what would happen afterward. Some of their friends who had married in their early twenties and had had children right away, ended up with disasterous results—marriage break-ups, children not well cared for, and confining lives. Tim and Sheryl didn't want their future to be like that. Fortunately, they were older and well established in their careers, and furthermore, they had some new friends who had just had their first child. There was no evidence of disasters. In fact, their friends were thriving; they were enjoying their infants and getting along well with each other. Encouraged by seeing their friends doing so well, Tim and Sheryl stopped taking birth control precautions and decided to let whatever happened happen. Shortly after, Sheryl suddenly felt very sick and jokingly concluded, "Either I'm dying of cancer or I'm pregnant."

Sheryl was accompanied by Tim when she went to her gynecologist to be tested. "When the doctor told me I was pregnant," said Sheryl, "I just about fainted. Then I went out in the waiting room and told Tim. He barely looked up and said, 'I told you so,' and just sat there as if he were mute." They soon left the office but for close to half an hour Tim still said nothing. "It took me quite a while to accept the fact that Sheryl was pregnant," said Tim, "and that there would be a third member of our family." Tim admits that he was excited about becoming a father but he was also troubled by the responsibilities he would be taking on and by the changes he would have to make.

## First Responses

Tim's response of excitement and apprehension is common and understandable. Some men have few reservations and openly rejoice when they first hear the news that they are to become fathers. At the other extreme are expectant fathers who, even though they may have expressed an interest and desire to have a child, are more upset or frightened than they are enthusiastic. These men need more time to grasp the full meaning of the reality of becoming a father.

Whether you responded to the news of your wife's pregnancy with great excitement, deep shock, or a mixture of both, you are about to experience one of the most exciting, challenging, and at times most frustrating periods of your life.

Until recently, the feelings an expectant father had during his wife's pregnancy were totally ignored. "Pregnancy and children," said Harvard psychologist Dr. Robert Fein, "have been seen as the property of mothers. Most people, including most social scientists and policy makers, have viewed men exclusively as breadwinners." I learned this personally in 1974, after my wife Kathy and I found out that she was pregnant with our first child. After the celebration, I figured that Kathy had her work cut out for her over the remaining eight months or so, but I hadn't the vaguest idea as to what was expected of me during this time or what role, if any, I was supposed to play. After all, I said to myself, the baby hadn't been immaculately conceived, there must be some important part for me, too.

Certainly there were clear challenges I had to face up to besides the immediate concern to earn enough money to support a child. Since I didn't have close friends who were fathers, I began searching through dozens of popular books on pregnancy and childbirth to learn about expectant fathers. To my dismay, I discovered that expectant fathers were treated superficially, if at all, and thus relegated to a state of limbo. It seemed that the world consisted only of mothers and children. Fathers were viewed as biological aids to conception who disappear after doing their job. Refusing to be discouraged, I kept searching for more information about expectant fathers. In the next few years I found that more and more researchers were beginning serious studies of expectant fathers and fathers of infants. In particular, they were examining the challenges these men face during the pregnancy period, what some of their needs are, and the impact they have on their wives and, later on, on their newborn children.

## Discovery and Acceptance

Soon after the news of your wife's pregnancy has been absorbed, you may find yourself reflecting seriously on the kind of father your father was to you. Dr. Robert Fein, a psychologist who conducted one of the first major studies of expectant fathers, claimed that, "For expectant fathers, pregnancy may precipitate some real searching and rethinking about experiences they had with their fathers and the ways in which they want to be a father to their children."

This period of reevaluation is a result of the radical change thrust upon you. For years, you've been a son, with all the conflicts that may have been associated with that role. These may have included competition with your father, possible dissatisfaction with your father for not giving you enough attention as a child, disappointment at not having lived up to his expectations, or failure to accept him, warts and all. With the birth of your own child, you may mull over in your mind these and lots of other father-child questions as you grapple with the question of what kind of father you want to be to your son or daughter. While you're becoming a father there still may be lingering and unresolved issues carried over from your own childhood and adolescence. But time is running out. Your primary position as son is about to end, and with it any vestiges of childhood that may remain such as the security of always having someone against whom to rebel or to measure yourself. Like generations of men before you, you may want to improve on your own father's performance. If your father was preoccupied with work in order to support the family and therefore was not home very much, you may not want to repeat that pattern. You also may want to resolve any conflicts still existing between you and your father. Now that you as son and father-to-be are faced with this new role, you may begin to see your father differently— less harshly, more compassionately—because, for the first time, you are about to step into your father's shoes. Wearing his shoes can help resolve conflicts if such exist or further deepen a relationship that has always been sound.

John Clift can serve as an example of what many men face on first learning they are to be fathers. Owner and manager of the Clift Collection, a Latin-American crafts and clothing store in Wellesley, Massachusetts, John grew up in the turbulent 1960s. He claims that the 1960s taught him that he did not have to play a rigid, stereotypic male role in which a man was expected to be constantly strong and to never express his deepest feelings.

When he learned of his wife's pregnancy, John reflected on what role his father had played as a father to him. His father had been a traditional father, primarily a breadwinner, and, as a result, said John, "I was never that close to my father when I was younger. But this has changed and I am becoming closer to him now." John Clift feels he has more options open to him than his father had some 30 years earlier. He would like a closer relationship with his child right from the start. "I want to be as close as I can with my child," said John. To bring this about, John redesigned his shop to include a nursery. Several months after his daughter, Lauren, was born, John's wife returned to work and John now takes care of Lauren while running his business.

Martin Paige's experience is similar to John Clift's. Martin feels that as a child he was much closer to his mother than to his father. His father, a practicing attorney, was busy establishing his career while his wife did most of the child care. Martin sees his father as being like most fathers of those years. "They thought babies were little things that should be shunted off until they put together coherent sentences. They also were afraid of babies." Now an expectant father for the first time, Martin, himself an attorney, wants to do things differently from his father. Thinking of his father's early role as a parent, Martin said, "I feel a lot of sadness when I think of my father then because I think he missed out a lot. I love my father very much. I'm sorry I wasn't as close to him earlier. Now I work with him and we're very close."

## Confusion and Change

While you are concerned about the question of what being a father means, at the very beginning of your wife's pregnancy you may also face a more immediate and pressing problem: how to deal with so many changes all at once. "At first a man may experience a great deal of excitement," said

Dr. Fein, "but he can also experience fear and anxiety." Enthusiastic over the news of his wife's pregnancy, a man may soon become baffled by the seemingly inexplicable changes she goes through. For up to 10 or 12 weeks, she may have morning sickness, become exhausted easily, and experience mercurial changes in mood.

Martin Paige found the first four or five months of his wife's pregnancy difficult to adjust to. When his wife Naomi told him she was pregnant, he was thrilled. "I have always wanted to be a father," he said. "Ever since I was a teenager I knew I wanted to have a family." But when he actually was an expectant father, it was different from what he had anticipated. Naomi began having morning sickness and was frequently drained and tired. "All of a sudden, I felt that I had lost my companion," said Martin. In order to survive this period, he was forced to assume an unfamiliar role: "I began paying more attention to how she felt. I tried to show her my love more spontaneously. I tried to be less selfish."

Unaccustomed to this new role, Martin was soon overwhelmed by it. By the time Naomi was four months pregnant, they were arguing frequently over petty things. It was a period of many stresses: Naomi had been fired from her job in a reshuffling of management; Martin was under heavy pressure at work. But most of all, he reflected later, he was not used to playing a nurturing role day in and day out. "I couldn't help feeling that it was a 'womanly' frame of mind," said Martin. "It was a role reversal that I wasn't ready for." After the arguing built up, he and Naomi finally moved on to what they should have begun with: frank and open discussions about the changes each was going through. Eventually the bickering ended.

Frank and open discussions are the best means of dealing with the confusion that can be associated with this initial period of pregnancy. It can be extremely difficult, however, to engage in rational discussion when both you and your wife are facing so many changes all at once. You may be perplexed by the extreme mood changes your wife may experience, and by her frequent fatigue and nausea.

Besides being tired and moody, a pregnant woman may not want to engage in any form of sexual activity because she's feeling so rotten. This, most likely, is temporary and easy to explain and understand, knowing how she feels. Nevertheless, you may find the lack of sex difficult to accept. To do so, you may have to play a more supportive role and more strongly express your care and affection. For some men, this comes close to a role reversal, a very difficult thing to do if they are more accustomed to receiving than giving affection. Said one expectant father, "I've always depended on my wife's care and support, but when she became pregnant, the pins were knocked out from under her. She was exhausted, she cried a lot. I feared I was going to have to care for her and eventually, the baby."

Adhering to a stereotypic role of breadwinner is inappropriate when your wife needs a different kind of support. True, she knows that you are hard at work advancing your career and making decisions that will assure financial security for your new family, but this will not help her during early pregnancy. During those weeks she may be nauseous in the mornings or so tired at the end of the day that she can't do anything but rest. Like you, she is worried about the relationship she wants to establish with her child. But mostly, she is overwhelmed with the nagging feeling that for eight or nine months she'll never once feel well, and beyond those months of fatigue lies an unknown future.

It should be stressed that these symptoms of early pregnancy are not universal, but neither are they uncommon. Many women manage to take in stride the discomfort that may accompany early pregnancy, and try not to permit the periodic symptoms of the first 10 or 12 weeks to interfere with their day-to-day responsibilities. What often helps them cope even better are empathetic husbands who can offer some extra support when it's needed. "An expectant father is needed to give all the support and strength and empathy he can," observed childbirth authority Elisabeth Bing, "but he must be encouraged to do so because our culture does not support this type of behavior in a man."

Describing how he had done a turnabout when his wife became pregnant, John Clift said, "I felt myself becoming more like a woman." He felt pressured into being more nurturing—more caring, more giving, more supportive—because his wife needed this help. At first, he viewed his behavior as womanly or feminine, but later he accepted it as part of him, concluding that there indeed was a strong nurturant side of every man.

Martin Paige talked about a similar transition he made soon after his wife became pregnant. "I had to pay a great deal of attention to my wife. I needed to support her, to show her my love. I had to learn to be more spontaneous in showing her how I felt and how much I cared for her." Martin felt he had to make some radical changes in his life. "I had to assume a womanly frame of mind. It was sort of a role reversal."

## New Roles

You too, may feel uncomfortable at first if you find your wife needs extra support. By being more nurturant, you are going against the culture, though not against nature. The concept of manliness or masculinity is embedded in our psyches and is primarily identified with doing (active, action), and the concept of womanliness or femininity, also deeply embedded in our psyches, is primarily identified with being (passive, inaction).

In our society males and females have been segregated according to what they did and how they did it, segregated, it must be added, in ways that have denied each a part of their true nature. As a result, masculinity was further defined and rigidly interpreted as strong, powerful, aggressive, forceful, active; and femininity, as passive, gentle, weak, and soft. These sharply contrasting descriptions of masculinity and femininity are becoming less valid now that many women are primary breadwinners and are gaining employment in traditionally male-dominated fields, while men are showing greater involvement with family life and child rearing. Dr. Fein tells a story illustrating one way some men have quietly redefined masculine and feminine as it applies to roles. It's a story of an expectant father who viewed fathers as the sole support of their families and mothers as those who care exclusively for the children. "This man," said Fein, "made it clear before the birth of his child that he wasn't going to have anything to do with this stuff. His wife would take care of the baby. Well, it turned out his wife had twins. And when I went to interview them six weeks after the birth, he was holding one baby in one arm and one baby in the other arm. 'He's having a love affair with the babies,' his wife said. 'He holds them and changes them, and thinks of them and feeds them. Helping out has made him a more loving man.'"

Many psychologists studying expectant fathers and fathers of infants are careful not to insist that there's one set way of acting as an expectant father or father of a newborn. According to Dr. Michael Yogman, "Fathers have to do what they feel comfortable in doing as fathers." This is echoed by University of Illinois research psychologist Dr. Ross Parke: "There is a variety of roles that fathers can choose to play."

No matter how you decide to respond to the circumstances surrounding the early stages of your wife's pregnancy or what role you've chosen to play, two things are quite clear to psychologists and other observers of expectant fathers. First, it is necessary to offer your wife support and encouragement as needed, and second, it is critical at the outset to communicate openly and freely with your wife about what each of you is experiencing. If the communication isn't open, the results may be disasterous—either immediately or in the long run.

When Dennis Merrimac's wife, Louise, first became pregnant, Dennis was excited and very optimistic about the prospect of becoming a father. But it soon turned out he got more than he had bargained for. Louise lost her job as a school teacher shortly after they learned she was pregnant, and Dennis worried excessively about his new financial responsibilities and was uncomfortable in playing a more nurturant role during those early months when Louise needed lots of extra attention. "I muddled through those early months," said Dennis, "and failed to offer all the support Louise needed." The results were nearly disasterous. Because of their poor communication, Louise and Dennis glossed over the feelings and concerns that bothered them the most. Louise was upset about losing her teaching position and resented Dennis's lack of understanding about how she was feeling. Dennis said he wanted to be an active father once the baby was born, but deep down he wanted Louise to play a more traditional role.

When their son was born, their communication problems grew worse. "We had moved to a small town in Maine," says Dennis, "and Louise increasingly felt trapped and isolated at home with the baby. Besides, there were not even any part-time jobs to be had for her." After months of harboring resentments and constant bickering, Dennis and Louise went to a marriage counselor and with his help were finally able to face up to their problems. Gradually and painfully, over the course of a year, they successfully resolved their major differences.

## Jealousy and Sharing

The experience of being an expectant father is a profoundly emotional one. Some men try to resist the experience by escaping. Dr. Libby Colman, coauthor of *Pregnancy: The Psychological Experience,* said "that some expectant fathers deal with it by running away, by acting in stereotypic masculine ways. They may take on an extra job, for example, because the provider role is the only one society has furnished for them." Other men deal with the experience as directly and as best as they can. How you are affected by it varies in as many ways as there are expectant fathers. But there are two rather dramatic ways in which some men respond: First, the father experiences distinct physical symptoms related to pregnancy, and second, he experiences jealousy.

Some expectant fathers suffer weight gain, loss of appetite, back pain, nausea, and stomach distress when their wives are pregnant. Obstetricians are sometimes asked by expectant fathers, "Doctor, am I supposed to be gaining as much weight as my wife?" Ludicrous though this question may sound, it points to how strongly affected some men are by the pregnancy of their wives. In one major study of expectant fathers in Great Britain, close to one out of every five fathers showed physical symptoms that were related to his wife's pregnancy. Researchers call this phenomenon the couvade syndrome after the practices of several Pacific Island, South American, and African tribes. *Couvade* (from the French *couver*, to brood or hatch) is used to describe a ritualistic role for fathers during the birth of their children. In these tribal rituals, a father mimics the motions of his wife as she goes through labor and delivery. By going through this elaborate process, the father vicariously experiences childbirth in such a way as to ward off any evil spirits that may harm his wife and their baby. It's a formal way for him to share more deeply in the experience of his child's birth by playing an equally important role; as a result, he does not feel left out.

Another way you may be affected by your wife's pregnancy is in feeling jealous. According to Dr. Colman, it is very rare for expectant fathers to even admit that they are jealous of their wives. But jealousy may often be present, especially if you are accustomed to receiving more than your fair share of your wife's attention and affection. Suddenly, your wife is the center of attention: she's carrying the baby, and friends, relatives, parents, and neighbors characteristically shower her with their concern, while you, whose attention she also needs and may at times demand, sink into the background.

One expectant father complained about his wife: "Erin had an awful lot of people pay attention to her. It was sister Erin, Aunt Erin, sister-in-law Erin, daughter Erin. It was something I didn't need at that time." Another father, when asked whether he felt any jealousy during his wife's pregnancy, said, "I feel very jealous. I think pregnancy is this great event—you walk around as though you have a gold star pinned on your chest. Actually, I'd like to have the baby. I don't want to be female, but I just feel left out. I feel fathers have been left out during pregnancy. It's a drag. My wife talks to her mother and her friends about it for hours and hours. It's as if men have no connection at all with pregnancy." Researchers call these responses "Zeus jealousy," a father's jealousy of the unborn child and of his wife's ability to bear a child. In greek mythology Zeus was the king of gods. He was so disturbed by a prophecy that his pregnant wife, Metis, was to bear a son who would rule the world that he swallowed her up. A birth nevertheless took place: Athene, the goddess of wisdom, sprung from the head of Zeus. This story and the ritualistic practices of couvade can be interpreted as ways in which expectant fathers have expressed their need to participate more actively in pregnancy.

According to Dr. Fein, there's too much emphasis on a father's envy of his wife and his unborn child. As a result, the positive side of what a father experiences is overlooked. "Of course, there's some envy there," admitted Dr. Fein. "Being pregnant is one of the few experiences that only women can have. But rather than overemphasize the jealousy, I take the position that men want to share in the experience. The more they can, the less they will envy, because they will feel less excluded."

# Fears

Expectant mothers have a variety of fears associated with their being pregnant. What often is overlooked is that their husbands, being expectant fathers, may have fears of their own.

### Economic Fears
Will I be able to support my wife and my child adequately? Should I get a second job? Is this the time to make that move to seek a promotion? Do I have enough money saved for an emergency? Is our health insurance adequate? These are just a few of the questions that reflect a concern for the economics of having a child. One of the reasons that the economic fear is such a major one is that traditionally the burden of finance rested solely on the shoulders of fathers. Thus, if you see yourself primarily as a breadwinner and cannot imagine a role that combines a career and playing a more active, nurturant role as a father, the economic pressure will be more difficult for you. About fathers facing such a dilemma, Dr. Colman said, "He has no im-

age of how to both go out and earn a living and take care of his child. The provider role is the dominant image he sees in society. If a man makes an active choice that he also wants to be a nurturant father, he's up against the society because there are no adequate role models." Now that more and more women are returning to work after they have children, there may be less economic pressure on men. Less pressure will help them to play two roles equally well—as a coprovider and as a nurturant father.

## Fears about Attending the Birth

If I attend the birth, will I be able to make it through okay? Will I be able to stand all the messier aspects of the birth? Will I faint? Elisabeth Bing, one of the world's best known childbirth educators, teaches 500 couples each year in her childbirth classes. According to Bing, fathers have many fears like those expressed in the above question. "Their fears," said Bing, "run from 'I fear seeing my wife suffer' and 'I faint at the sight of blood' to 'I don't like hospitals.' Unfortunately, they all have images of buckets of blood." If you have such fears, they are usually overcome once you are exposed to a good childbirth education course. There you will learn what to expect at the birth itself and how you can assist your wife. You will meet other fathers with fears similar to yours, and during the four- to ten-week course, you will start to feel more comfortable about the idea of attending your child's birth.

Richard Retblatt of New York told his wife he didn't want to be there when their first child was born. And he certainly didn't want to go to the childbirth education classes. Under pressure from his wife, he reluctantly took the course and some of his fears were allayed, yet he still wasn't particularly excited by the course. He finally decided to be there with his wife during labor and delivery. He is thankful things turned out the way they did. About the birth of his daughter, Richard said, "I would say it was one of the biggest thrills of my life. I would have been depressed if I hadn't gone." Elisabeth Bing said that almost all the fathers she's known who have been reluctant at first wind up being most enthusiastic and surprised to find out their fears were unfounded.

## Fears about Your Marital Relationship

Will the baby interfere with our lives? Will I take a second place to the baby in my wife's affections? Will we make a smooth transition to parenthood? Will I be tied down?

Anytime one is faced with a major change such as becoming a father—having a third person permanently join a two-person relationship—there are accompanying fears regarding the suspected or unknown. In a recent report of a study of expectant parents, a team of researchers at the University of California at Berkeley concluded that expectant parents experience some disequilibrium during pregnancy. But if they are close to one another, are open with one another in communicating what each is experiencing, couples are better able to make the transition to parenthood. If their relationship to each other is solid, the unsettling nature of becoming parents, of adjusting to their changed life-styles, proves to be an opportunity for growth and for the regeneration of their relationship. This is what Richard and Emily Lewis of Arkansas experienced during Emily's pregnancy. They felt they came closer together, and that the pregnancy served to help them grow, culminating in not just the birth of their child but in the birth of their family. "When our daughter Addy was born," said Richard, "I felt it was a beautiful completion of our marriage, of our family."

If there are major strains in their relationship, expectant parents can seek help through individual or group counseling. Very often the tensions and conflicts that ordinarily arise can be effectively reduced through childbirth preparation programs, which give men and women the opportunity to discuss major issues they will confront both before and after the birth. (See chapter 6 for more on childbirth preparation.)

## Fears about Sexual Relations

Is it safe to have intercourse during pregnancy? Will I hurt the baby while making love? Will my wife be turned off by sex throughout her pregnancy? These are just a few of the questions commonly asked.

Sexual activity is acceptable, safe, and encouraged during normal, healthy pregnancies. You may have to adapt to circumstances: Your sexual activity may be curtailed during pregnancy, especially at the beginning and near the end of the nine months. Some women experience an increased desire for sexual activity during pregnancy; some women experience a sharp decrease in sexual interest; and some women experience positive and negative feelings about sexual activity at various times. Be prepared to experience changes in how both of you communicate sexually—changes in both frequency and quality. Both your understanding and experience of sex may indeed be expanded.

After the initial awkwardness he felt during the first few months of his wife's pregnancy, John Clift discovered that the quality of his sexual relationship with his wife actually improved: "Being attentive to each other was just as important as making love. We don't always have to have intercourse. I've always known this, but Karen's pregnancy has just made it easier to be open about it." (For a more detailed discussion of sexual relations during pregnancy, see chapter 4.)

# A Father's Most Exciting Moments

The changes, fears, and doubts a father may face during pregnancy are overshadowed, in the long run, by the most exciting and rewarding aspects of being an expectant father—falling in love with the growing realization that you will soon be a father and sharing deeply in the experience of your wife's pregnancy. One of the earliest dramatic moments when this realization becomes evident occurs around the fourth or fifth month. Your wife is feeling very good, having successfully met the challenges of the first few months, and now the baby inside is gaining weight and strength rapidly. The baby is no longer an abstraction. Around this time many expectant parents begin calling him or her by name, usually a humorous, interim name that is used until the baby makes its appearance and is formally named.

The baby starts to be noticeably active: At first only the mother can notice any movement, which usually takes the form of a fluttering motion. By the sixth month, fluttering turns into a mild rumbling that you can observe and feel when you place your hand on your wife's abdomen. There are some babies, however, who won't budge when their fathers try to make contact, so don't be disappointed if this happens to you. For a mother, the baby's activity is special; she begins to identify with him or her, drawing closer and closer. According to Dr. Marshall Klaus, Professor of Pediatrics at Case Western University School of Medicine, many mothers start falling in love with their babies during this period before the birth. Says Klaus, "Thirty percent of mothers fall in love with their babies before they're born, 30 percent fall in love with them after they've held them skin to skin, and 40 percent fall in love with them over the next four to six weeks. In other words, you don't have instant bonding. This form of attachment toward infants is not instant glue." Unfortunately, few observers ever talk about fathers falling in love with their babies, particularly before their babies are born. Dr. James Hahn, Chief of Obstetrics and Gynecology at Lexington County Hospital in West Columbia, South Carolina, thinks fathers have been overlooked. "A father can definitely begin relating to his child antenatally," said Dr. Hahn. This is precisely what many fathers are doing.

Talking about his wife's pregnancy and how he felt about their child growing inside, one expectant father said, "Up to the third month, it's been like a strange kind of growth. But now it's more personal. It's like a sleeping child. You can see it move and you can feel it. In fact, there's nothing so exciting as to have your wife lie against your back and feel the baby move." Another expectant father carried the thought further: "In every way I try to visualize what the baby's like inside her, and I try to visualize her face, her hair, her fingernails. I try to visualize and feel her every move." Another father, Richard Lewis, said that he and his wife Emily would spend hours feeling their daughter's movements and talking to her, especially during the three months prior to her birth. Richard talked about his sense of being very much involved. "I felt very close to her even then." Even in utero she had a personality of her own, quite an active one. I also felt very close to Emily. There was a different way of caring about her that I had never felt before. I used to put my hand on Emily's belly and the baby would stretch. All of a sudden you could feel her elbow. I was nervous when I first started feeling the baby. Emily wasn't so nervous, though. After doing it for a while, I loved it."

During playful moments when you gently feel your child in the womb and sense the dramatic and awe-inspiring life readying to burst forth soon, you will begin to get a deeper feeling of the sheer excitement of what it means to become a father. When you and your wife share your innermost thoughts and feelings about your child, you will be drawn closer and closer together. The ultimate manifestation of this closeness, of your love for one another, will be the birth of your child.

# Diary of an Expectant Father

*I've kept a journal for years, writing in it mostly during the more dramatic moments in my life. While Kathy was pregnant with our son Geoffrey, I made entries in my journal during the first two months and during the seventh, eighth, and ninth month of pregnancy. I had not set out to keep a regular account of what was happening to me throughout pregnancy. It turned out that there was more upheaval in my life as a result of the pregnancy during these months than during the middle months. In the middle months, life was fairly tranquil. It was more hectic when Kathy first became pregnant and extremely hectic the month or so before the birth because we were going to move back to New England immediately afterward. Being more affected during these times by all the changes we faced, I wrote about them.*

### December 4

Kathy's three weeks late with her period. We want to get pregnant but wonder if it's just a missed period. What a week for this to happen! Kathy's feeling sick. Kristen's sick and has had a fever for two days. We've been up all night with her a couple of times this week. And all of us are still exhausted from our 18-hour train ride from Boca Raton, where we recently visited Dad and Helena.

### December 11

Kathy trudges up the stairs at 1:30 this afternoon. Standing by the phone, I turn to greet her, hoping, trying to keep cool. Kathy pauses for a few seconds, then smiles exuberantly, and says, "Well, it's Papa No. 2." We embrace. Tears well up in my eyes. I am beside myself with joy. "But is it for sure?" I ask. "No, not for sure, not until a pelvic exam is taken."

### December 12

Kathy leaves for the appointment with the doctor, returns at noon. I return at 1:15 P.M. "It's for sure. But guess what?" Kathy says. "The doctor thinks we might have twins. He's not certain, but he was so excited himself that he called in Dr. Hahn to examine me. We'll know for sure during the next visit—in two or three weeks when he listens to heartbeats." Kathy and I are very excited—a bit nervous as well. One baby at a time is demanding enough, but how do you manage with two? But there's no history of twins in either of our families. We both find the prospect of twins terribly exciting, but we'll be happy with just one healthy baby—boy or girl. Deep down inside I hope it's a boy. But I find a boy scary. Why? It would make me rethink my relationship with Dad—my disappointment at not being very gifted musically as he is, at not fulfilling whatever it is sons are to fulfill. Sometimes I still wonder if I really know what I want to do, except make enough money to do my share to raise a family. And that hasn't been easy. But right now I am on the verge of doing some things, making some money.

About being an expectant father again: Kathy needs my added support—she's very tired, needs lots of sleep and is queasy frequently. I'm trying to do more around the house, to do more with Kristen, but I must try even harder. Most important thing for Kathy is rest, freedom from worry, and good food. I'm very happy about becoming a father for the second time, but I'm also apprehensive at times about bringing another person onto this troubled planet! The advantages, however, of being alive outweigh the disadvantages. To be alive today is still terribly exciting. It beats all other alternatives.

### December 25

We've traveled north for Christmas in New England. This is Kristen's fourth Christmas and it's a delight to watch her having such a good time. I tell her how much I love her, how beautiful she is, and how very special she is to me. I don't ever want how I feel about her to go unsaid.

Some things I don't want to forget: I'm more involved now—I know more and have a greater empathy for how Kathy feels during these first weeks of pregnancy (which is rotten on many occasions, queasy, tired, wiped out) and so I'm getting up in the middle of the night to take Kristen to the bathroom when she needs to go; I'm often getting Kristen ready for bed, bathing her, helping her brush her teeth, and I'm generally enjoying it. I never liked doing these things before. I was lazy and let Kathy do all the routine child-care duties. But now it's different, although it sometimes is still a bit of a struggle, but it's the least I can do, for I really think fathers should be active parents and not leave everything to mothers. Leaving things to mothers has taken its toll: Look at some of the people I know and witness the alienation between them and their fathers. This seems to be greater between fathers and sons. There's usually a superficial show of affection and respect between the two but there's often no real communication.

My hunch is that if fathers took a more active role (did more, helped more, shared more with their kids), everyone would be better off. And this "doing more" starts before a child is born—when he's thrashing around in the womb.

### December 29

We're visiting New York for the New Year's weekend. Kathy still feels wiped out. We've done so much traveling in the past week. She needs to go easy, mustn't overdo. I just read Ashley Montagu's book on prenatal life and was impressed with the fact that this is the most critical time in the development of our baby (its brain is forming now) so Kathy needs plenty of rest and lots of good food. I'm much more conscious this time of my responsibility as a provider. When the baby is born, Kathy wants to take a six-month leave of absence. To do this, I must find a better-paying job. Must start hustling. Must follow up on job contacts. I wish Kathy were feeling better. I don't like celibacy, even though I know it's only temporary. She should feel better soon.

### May 16

I've neglected my journal for months. Kathy's doing very well. She's getting lots of exercise, she swims about 1/4 mile every day, and she's looking forward to the baby.

Whenever she gets worried about the birth, I remind her about how well she did when Kristen was born and that she will do well again and that there's only one way to look at pregnancy—positively.

During the last month or so, when we've made love, a curious phenomenon has occurred. (Sometimes I feel that making love itself is not so much curious as a rare phenomenon recently, since we've not been making love as often as we did when Kathy was pregnant with Kristen. This is because Kathy is working and we've got Kristen to take care of, which doesn't leave Kathy with much extra energy at the end of the day. They don't tell you these things in the pregnancy books.) The curious phenomenon is how the baby shifts. At first, both Kathy and I got worried about it. My weight on Kathy—on the baby, too—seemed to flatten the baby out. Suddenly it looked as if Kathy wasn't pregnant anymore. Her stomach was flattened. We were amazed that this could happen, but got used to it once we began looking more carefully, noticing all kinds of subtle shifts, all of which we eventually realized were normal.

Since the sixth month, when Kathy started getting bigger and bigger, she occasionally gets tired of her new shapeless figure. I kid her about it, calling her "Your Immenseness" or "Your Hugeness" and when she gets stuck in a low lounge chair, which has happened once or twice, I tell her she's in need of a derrick. She takes it all good naturedly. I try not to overdo it, though, because of the sensitive nature of pregnancy. It must be difficult for women who've grown up with the idea of having to maintain a thin figure to be pregnant. Sometimes they lose some self-esteem due to their unshapely figures.

### May 23

Two months to go till D-day. Last night Kathy was very upset, complained of being trapped; she's teaching summer school at the university, a three-week session, and helping several students who are doing independent study with her. Also, South Carolina's weather has been oppressive. Kathy just wants to be away from here. Is there more? I ask. "I wish you could understand how it feels to be pregnant," Kathy says. I try but it's hard. It makes me sad I can't do more. "You don't seem to mind being here; you're working on your book. I'm tired, I've been working all year. I just want a vacation." Kathy broke down in tears. I've been so preoccupied with finishing a piece for *Glamour* and working on my book. I feel torn in two directions. Just at the time I need to spend so much time working, Kathy needs me more. There's more. Worries and fears. The oppressive heat, the teaching, taking care of Kristen. With so many responsibilities, Kathy's concerned about the baby's health, about doing everything she has to do. I try to assure her how remarkable she actually is and that she shouldn't worry so much. I keep trying and trying to empathize, to offer what encouragement I can, but, damn, it's hard. Sometimes I feel helpless, but fortunately when I do say very positive things to Kathy and when I do more around the house or spend more time with Kristen, Kathy seems to feel a lot better. These moments of worry, thank God, are infrequent, because Kathy is generally upbeat and positive in her thinking, and she very much looks forward to the birth of the baby.

### May 25

Last night I started reading a scientific account of pregnancy and it struck me how mysterious and magical and beautiful the process of birth is. I feel I'm very ignorant about what happens and I want to learn more, to read more. Was impressed with Dr. Hahn's remark about fathers and antenatal bonding. A father, he said, can also begin feeling close to his child before the child is born. Kathy says most of the books she's read about pregnancy always talk about how women start to identify with their children in the womb. She says she feels attached to the baby way before it's born.

At supper tonight I told Kristen about the baby's heartbeat. I was struck by the fact that two heartbeats are within Kathy. "Strange," said Kathy, in a kidding tone of voice. Strange, yes, miraculous, actually. Kristen wanted to listen to the heartbeat, so we'll arrange to have her visit the doctor's office on Kathy's next check-up.

### May 26

I was so cranky today, it affected Kathy. I was upset about the work I have to get done, about the number of hours I'm putting in on my television show so I can have it shown on another station, and about not making enough money. It's not fair to upset Kathy like that.

### May 27

Kathy and I have been trying to prepare Kristen for her new baby sister or brother. Today, Kristen walked into the living room, pushed her stomach forward, and proudly announced, "Mama and Papa, I'm going to have a baby, too. Look, I have a baby in my stomach."

### May 31

We're in Massachusetts, staying at Kathy's father's house. Kathy is scheduled to be interviewed for a position in the art history department of a

New England college. She is seven months pregnant and looks it. This morning the following "incident" occurred. While Kathy was out walking, a pickup truck pulled up alongside her, and a young, good-looking, blond-haired man in his early twenties thrust his head out the window and called to Kathy, "I hope you don't think I'm being rude or anything, but you look beautiful." He smiled and then drove off down the road. Kathy was quite amused by the incident. I agreed with the man's assessment. Kathy is beautiful, pregnant or not pregnant, but because of ingrained prejudices about pregnant women, I am constantly surprised to realize how attractive, physically, sexually attractive, Kathy and many other pregnant women are. I used to think it heresy to think this way, but I have found many men who agree with me. The man in the pickup truck is obviously one of them.

Kathy and I are talking a lot about the baby now. It's more than just a possibility. S/he moves around alot. (I like the way the International Childbirth Education Association often refers to someone who may be a she or he with "s/he".) Kathy has been preparing Kristen for the baby very thoughtfully and lovingly. I help as much as I can. When I asked Kristen today if she is going to help take care of her new baby brother or sister, she smiled and said, "Yes." She then ran downstairs to her bedroom and showed me the baby clothes she and Kathy had arranged to take back to South Carolina. She was already helping to prepare for the baby.

Nights are a special time during pregnancy. Kathy and I talk about the baby, then kid about the baby, and I sometimes gently run my hand across Kathy's abdomen to feel any movements. But nights can also be trying. When the day is done and night falls, fears and worries stalk us from time to time. Last night at 10:30 Kathy called to me, "Sean, I need some reassurance, tell me everything's going to be okay. I'm so worried. Do you think the baby's all right?" I hugged her, saying, "Of course, everything's going to be all right. The baby's going to be fine." I said this in a very soothing tone of voice, almost as if I was stroking her with my voice. Kathy felt better immediately.

### June 1

We had a great time "playing" with the baby tonight. I stroked Kathy's stomach and gently felt the baby. I felt strong movement: It felt as if the baby was swinging his elbows to get some more room.

I told Kathy about an interview I had with Dr. Michael Yogman today. He said a friend of his talks to his baby in utero. I thought that was a terrific idea, so I began talking to our baby tonight. Feeling a bit strange about the whole idea of talking to an unborn baby, I started off in a joking manner. "Hello, down there, whoever you are. This is your father speaking. I just learned from Michael Yogman, M.D., who works a lot with babies and fathers, that his friend used to speak to his baby before it was born. It dawned on me I've missed out on something, so I thought we'd have a little chat. So here goes." I soon became serious, though, and I decided it wasn't such a crazy idea to converse like this. "Baby Gresh," I continued, "I want you to know that your mother, Kathy, is a bit worried about you. I think you're fine and going to have a good birth. Now about your mama. Once you get to know her, you'll get to love her, as I do. She's a terrific woman. She tends to worry a little bit too much at times, but that's okay—it gives us a chance to kid around more and we just turn those worries upside down. When you get to know her, you'll love her. Actually, it's silly to say 'when you get to know her' because you know her more intimately already than anyone can imagine because you're so close to her. She's been doing well by you, taking very good care of you—very good care indeed—exercising, eating well, planning for you. I'm real excited about your being, and am a little bit worried, too, because of all the changes that'll take place after you're born. Kathy and I are trying to change jobs now but despite this bit of unsettlement, I'm very optimistic things will be terrific for you, for all of us. I've never been more confident, more excited, more hopeful. By the way, not incidentally, Kristen's your big sister: Like you, she was where you are now a few years ago. She's a terrific little girl, so gentle and sweet and bright and dear and everything good you can imagine. You'll love her too. She'll love you and is excited about your coming. Crazy, isn't it, to say 'your coming,' since you're here already. Sorry I haven't been talking to you before, I'll make up for it. Talk to you again, and I'll be in touch with you soon. In the meantime, please be well."

### June 24

The baby is due in four weeks. Today, looking at Kathy, I tried to picture the baby growing and moving inside her, exercising his lungs and flexing his arms and legs so awkwardly. Then I thought of the birth and the trauma some people say the baby will go through during birth. I thought of the labor and how difficult it is and how courageous Kathy will have to be again, as she was when Kristen was born. I thought of my position as an observer, a father, who is also responsible for this baby's existence yet is unable to take on or share some of the strain of childbirth.

### July 15

Two weeks, more or less, to go. We're finally getting down to choosing names. So far it's Ian for a boy and Ashley for a girl. Other names are still in the running, however: Geoffrey and Deidre head up a small list of possible choices.

### July 16

Kathy accepted the offer to teach this fall in New England. This means that the summer will bring a new baby, a new home, new jobs, a new region of the country. We will be registering high up on the stress scale regarding all the changes we'll face at the same time. We're determined to survive it all.

Today I listed all the things worrying me. If I look at the worries as challenges, I may handle them better.

I'm worried about the contract we signed with someone who wants to purchase our house, about getting a suitable house in Massachusetts, about meeting the deadline for my book, about having enough money after the baby is born to hire someone to help us a few hours a day so both of us can work. Now I must turn these worries into positive forces, into challenges. Knowing the problems I face, I will now attack them realistically and use my time more efficiently, decide on my priorities, and adapt.

Enough of these concerns. Kathy's observations tonight helped me keep all these things in perspective. While we were lying in bed reading, out of the blue, Kathy said, "I think he's got big feet."

"Who's got big feet," I asked.

"The Baby."

"How do you know?"

"Because he's kicking so much, and his feet are showing right through. Here, look."

## July 19

At 5:30 this morning, I was downstairs getting ready to start writing when Kathy rushed in, very upset. She had been dreaming about chemicals coming from the ground and threatening the baby. She was afraid. She had also dreamt that Kristen's life, too, was in danger. I came back to bed with her, reassured her that dreams like these are natural and understandable. They showed how much she really loved the children and how deep was her concern for them.

It turns out that several days before, Kathy had read a magazine article about a town in Michigan that had several chemical plants, and was threatened by mysterious disasters and diseases. I think it influenced her dream. It just added fuel to the fire, that is, to the natural fears any expectant mother has about her child. I told Kathy of the fears I sometimes have about Kristen, fears that she might die suddenly, fears that make me very sad because I love her so much and think the world of her. Kathy and I lay there in bed for over an hour, snuggled against each other. I could feel Kathy's stomach pressed tightly against my side. I felt the very strong movements of the baby—he or she seemed unaffected by the dreams and seemed to be flailing his arms and legs vigorously, a reassuring sign to both of us he was thriving, preparing to make his entrance soon.

## July 20

If we have a boy, will I feel pressured to make sure I am a strong figure for him to model himself on? Why does the prospect of having a boy make me even think of questions like this?

## July 22

Tension builds. The baby's due date is tomorrow, and the doctor says the birth may be within the next two weeks.

# Considerations for Expectant Fathers

*To be a more involved expectant father, consider the following:*

1. Sharing your thoughts, feelings, joys, and fears with your wife is critical for making a smoother transition to fatherhood. The sharing *must be mutual*, for both of you are going through many changes all at once. Studies have shown that the closer a man and woman are, and the more open with each other they are about their experiences during pregnancy, the smoother the transition they will make to parenthood.

2. Visit the obstetrician-gynecologist with your wife as often as you can, at least two or three times. Ask the doctor all the questions you want and together work out the details regarding the birth, that is, the childbirth method your wife and you have decided to follow.

3. Talk to other supportive fathers. Men generally don't have networks of people with whom they can freely discuss what they are going through as expectant fathers. Therefore, it may be necessary for you to go out of your way to meet some men who are or have been expectant fathers. If you haven't met anyone during the early stages of your wife's pregnancy, you'll have plenty of opportunity if you decide to attend childbirth preparation classes.

4. As the baby becomes more and more active in the womb, take time to feel him or her move, to watch the immediate activity, and to discuss with your wife her feelings about what's happening with the baby.

5. During your wife's pregnancy, offer her the extra support she needs: emotional support by way of encouragement and physical support of doing many of the household tasks she may ordinarily do. This all boils down to being sensitive to her feelings and needs, and acting accordingly. The more comfortable she is, the less anxiety she has, the better she'll feel, and the better the baby will be.

6. Work out details regarding what roles each of you will be playing as parents. Traditional roles or more sharing ones are both valid and acceptable, as long as both of you are clear which you are to play. Not deciding what your responsibilities will be leads to confusion later on.

7. Read as much as you can about pregnancy and childbirth and about newborns and reflect on what you read. But most important, act on your own deepest instincts. Despite what you may read about the latest trend, trust your feelings and act accordingly.

# 3

# What's Ahead for Expectant Mothers

Three months after she gave birth to her second child, Elizabeth talked about what it was like to be pregnant and how her husband responded to her experience. "My husband helped me a lot. He listened to me. He supported me. He tried to be empathetic. But I think it was hard for him. In fact, I think it is difficult for any man to empathize about being pregnant because he's not pregnant nor will he ever be." Elizabeth is typical of many women who are sensitive to the problems and challenges their husbands face during pregnancy. Reflecting on the position husbands find themselves in, she commented, "During pregnancy a husband shouldn't feel like he's being jilted or neglected. Of course, he's neglected to some extent because some of the energies you usually expend on him, you use in dealing with feeling sick and tired or just in taking extra time to do things. A husband shouldn't take all this personally. But wives shouldn't be overdemanding, either."

Although not taking things personally or not being a bit thrown off balance during your wife's pregnancy, especially during the first 10 or 12 weeks, is easier said than done, it is wise advice. The early stage of pregnancy is characterized by enormous physiological and emotional changes. In most cases, a woman will take these changes in stride; however, they often are unsettling and will add strain to her daily life. Fortunately, this period is short-lived and after the first two months or so, your wife will feel quite good.

She will feel much better, even during the very early weeks of her pregnancy, if you empathize with her, share with her your excitement about the pregnancy, and offer her your undivided support. By empathizing with her, seeing her situation from *her* perspective, you will be able to have a clearer understanding of how she feels. She, in turn, will have one less worry to deal with—the tension that could arise if you interpreted her occasional irritability, tiredness, or sudden change of mood as if it were directed against you. Early pregnancy is when the baby goes through the most critical period of prenatal development, and is significantly affected by how well the mother eats, how well rested she is, and how physically fit she is. Therefore, the baby will benefit if the mother is free of any unnecessary tension or worries.

To see things more from the pregnant woman's viewpoint, to be able to offer her encouragement and moral support when needed, and to have a positive influence on your developing child, it is important to consider first, the physiological changes a newly developing child experiences and the physiological changes that a woman undergoes at the same time, and second, some of the emotional changes a woman may face during pregnancy.

## The Physiological Changes

The physiological aspects of pregnancy and birth can be clinically and scientifically explained in fairly straightforward language. To know this language is important and very helpful. But the language points to a reality beyond the meaning of each clinical or scientific explanation. That reality is the mystery enveloping the entire process of pregnancy and birth. It is important not to lose a sense of this mystery in which you and your wife are now participating.

The first element of this mystery is the phenomenon of fertilization.* One mature spermatozoon (sperm cell), approximately 1/500 inch long, weighing a fraction of a millionth of an ounce, and looking like a pin with an oval head and a long thin tail, travels along with hundreds of millions of other spermatozoa at the speed of 1 inch every 16 to 20 minutes for a distance of up to 12 inches to the oviduct. There, after surviving this arduous journey, it penetrates the ovum (egg cell), which is 1/175 inch in diameter, weighs 1/20 of a millionth of an ounce, and can be fertilized for only a brief period of about 72 hours every month. Considering the fact that any one of more than 300 million sperm cells could ultimately unite with any one of the mother's 400 ova, the child who evolves could have been any one of over 100 billion entirely different persons. Considering the possibilities surrounding anyone's coming into being, the one in over 300 million chance that a sperm cell will survive the trip and unite successfully with a mature ovum, and considering the infinitesimal size of the two cells that eventually develop into a human being, there is beyond doubt a mystery that envelops the entire process, a mystery that cannot be put into dry, scientific terms.

You may initiate the process of pregnancy by making love to your wife in the mutual hope that she will get pregnant. But once fertilization occurs and pregnancy begins, the process is, for all intents and purposes, out of your control. This is true for your wife as well. She is now pregnant, and although what she eats, how rested and relaxed she is, and how she views her pregnancy all influence the developing child within her, she cannot willingly control the process of the developing life. Through a very complex process, the two cells united at conception in her body will grow in the next 240 to 300 days into a baby who will be 18 to 20 inches long, weigh approximately 7 pounds, and will consist of close to 200 billion cells. The growth is filled with drama and mystery, a point the English poet Samuel Taylor Coleridge stressed when he wrote more than a century ago, "The history of man for nine months preceeding his birth would, probably, be far more interesting, and contain events of greater moment, than all the threescore and ten years that follow it." It is a point worth remembering, especially when the drama outside the womb tends to absorb you.

### *The First 12 Weeks:* The First Trimester

Once the sperm cell unites with the ovum in the oviduct, the two cells form an embryo. Consisting of two cells with two nuclei, each containing 23 pairs of chromosomes (the hereditary elements), the embryo slowly begins moving down the oviduct toward the uterus. After about 36 hours, the two

---

*Roberts Rugh and Landrum B. Shettles. **From Conception to Birth: The Drama of Life's Beginnings.**

cells divide, thus beginning a complex process of mitosis or cell division that will eventually result in the hundreds of billions of cells that make up a human being. Between the seventh and ninth day, the embryo, which now consists of hundreds of cells, has reached the uterus and roots itself in its upper wall.

During the first three weeks, the embryo grows to about the size of a raisin. Although it doesn't resemble a human form yet, it contains the cellular beginnings of the spinal column, the nervous system, the circulatory system, and the major organs.

In the second week after fertilization, the placenta begins forming. This circular mass of tissues grows embedded in the uterus and functions as a conduit for the exchange of oxygen and nutrients between the mother and baby. The baby's blood, which never mingles with the mother's, is filtered through the placenta where oxygen and nutrients are picked up and waste products discharged. Forming at the same time as the placenta is the umbilical cord. It connects the embryo to the placenta and because the embryo will soon be floating within the amniotic sac, the cord is a flexible, jelly-like tube that eventually grows to a length of from 5 inches to as much as 4 feet.

By the end of the fourth week, the embryo is 1/4 inch long, consists of millions of cells, and is shaped like a soft, semicircular tube. It weighs about 1/30 ounce (1 gram), and, microscopic though it is, its heart begins to pulsate.

Around the eighth week, the embryo begins to take on a recognizably human form, and is called a fetus. Up to this stage it is difficult to tell the human embryo from that of an elephant, a chicken, or a goat, without examining its chromosomes microscopically. By the eighth week its wide-set eyes, lowered ears, and open mouth, which are still evolving, are distinctively human in appearance.

By the twelfth week, the fetus grows to about 3-1/2 inches in length and weighs about 2 ounces. It could fit snugly in the palm of your hand.

### *The Fourth, Fifth, and Sixth Months:* The Second Trimester

During this period, the baby continues his dramatic development. In the fourth month, he almost doubles in length and measures about 6 inches. He now weighs 4–6 ounces and as his skeleton grows stronger each day, he becomes slightly more erect. His facial features are becoming more refined—his eyes are closer together, his lips are more prominently shaped, and his ears are higher and more properly positioned. The heart is beating more demonstrably and is now circulating about 25 quarts of blood through the fetus' body every day. Through the use of a special stethoscope, you can hear the fetal heartbeat, between 120 to 160 beats a minute. During the fourth month, the baby's movements grow stronger as he starts stretching his arms and legs. These movements are barely noticed by the mother at this time but by the end of the fourth month or during the fifth month, the movements are stronger and definitely noticed. This activity is called quickening. During the fifth month, the baby grows a few more inches and almost doubles his weight in four or five weeks. He is now about 8 inches long and weighs 8–10 ounces (about half a pound). His body is now covered with a fine layer of hair. Although he's completely enveloped in the amniotic fluids and doesn't receive oxygen through any lung activity, his lungs will function from time to time, pumping the amniotic fluid in and out. This pumping occurs every 2 to 4 seconds and can last up to half an hour; a mother will describe it by saying her baby is hiccuping. Starting around the fifth month, the baby's pattern of activity may be clearly noticed. A mother can tell when her baby is sleeping and when he's awake: when he's moving about, stretching his arms and legs, when he's changing positions, and when he's restless. The baby is sensitive to touch now, and responds when one puts pressure on the mother's abdomen. Furthermore, he's sensitive to sound and can be startled by loud noises, or at least stirred if he hears loud music or noise.

By the sixth month, the baby's weight is triple what it was just four weeks before. He now weighs about 1-1/2 pounds and is 1 foot long. His body is elongated, a necessary position to allow space for his internal organs to develop, and his skin is reddish in color and protected by a gluelike coating. His grip is extremely strong during this stage, a trait thought to be inherited from simian ancestors who may have needed such a grip to survive. By the time he is born, the baby's grip won't be as strong, but were he born prematurely, his grip would be so strong that while he was clasping your index fingers with his two tiny hands, you could lift him entirely out of his crib.

### *The Seventh, Eighth, and Ninth Months:* The Third Trimester
The baby will gain about 5 pounds during the last three months and therefore space within the womb gets cramped. His movements are felt more strongly, especially when he moves his arms and legs. These movements cause sudden bulges in the mother's abdomen, which you can see and feel quite clearly.

In the seventh month, the baby is about 16 inches long and weighs about 3 pounds. Should the baby be born prematurely at this time, he could survive, although his chances would be approximately 40 to 50 percent. During the seventh month, the baby's brain and nervous system, which began to form during the third week after conception, begin a period of rapidly increased development.

By the eighth month, the baby weighs about 5 pounds and is 1-1/2 feet long. Should he be born now, he would have about a 70 percent chance of surviving because he is so close to full term in his prenatal development.

Finally, by the ninth month, the baby typically weighs about 7 pounds and is about 20 inches long. He is in an upside-down position and sometime around two weeks or so before the birth, his body drops an inch or two and his head becomes engaged in the lower region of the pelvic area.

# The Emotional Changes

"Women," said Elisabeth Bing, "are in either one of two states of health: pregnant or not pregnant." Unfortunately, when a woman becomes pregnant, many people tend to view her as being "sick," not fully healthy. Consequently, stereotypic images of a pregnant woman prevail in many people's minds: A pregnant woman is sick, frequently tired, unstable, cries a lot, is easily upset, is prone to strange cravings. In short, the stereotype is of an irrational female.

## Hormones and Feelings

The truth of the matter is that pregnancy is a condition of normal health. It is a normal, though complex, biological process, which can be confused with a condition of sickness because it may be accompanied by symptoms commonly associated with ill health. If you keep in mind the incredible, dramatic, and awesome changes going on within a woman from the time of conception, you will be able to get a better understanding as to how these changes may be affecting her physically and emotionally.

When a woman becomes pregnant, she experiences a great number of physical changes brought about by increased amounts of the hormones progesterone and estrogen. Although the onset of pregnancy is a major biological change in all expectant mothers, reactions to it vary widely. Some women are very little affected by it and during the first 10 to 12 weeks of pregnancy, the period when a pregnant woman can be most susceptible to the biological changes, they are barely aware that they are pregnant. Other women are mildly affected by the changes during the first trimester and may feel unusually tired and, occasionally, nauseated. Some women, however, are greatly affected by the changes taking place in their bodies during early pregnancy. They frequently feel miserable, may become extremely fatigued, have periods of nausea, are generally irritable, and experience mercurial mood changes.

As a woman's body adjusts to host this new being, the involuntary changes it goes through are reflected in symptoms that may unnerve her. She may be bewildered by them and perplexed if you are unsympathetic to how she feels. "I was very irritable during the first weeks of my pregnancy," said Laura. "This could have been partly attributable to my anxiety, because I had already had two miscarriages, but it was also due to the hormonal changes. I remember it very clearly. It was an unexplained irritability, like I was sometimes out of control. I felt ashamed that I felt this way." Laura said this experience of being so oversensitive didn't last long, but it was disturbing. "My husband," she continued, "was baffled by the experience and he tried very hard to understand." Laura and her husband argued a lot during this time, something Laura feels could have been avoided. "I think keeping the lines of communication open is the most important thing. We should have discussed our feelings. I think he felt left out because I was getting all kinds of attention and nurturing from everybody." About the situation of husbands during the early stage of pregnancy and about her husband in particular, Laura said, "I think men should understand that some unpredictable things are going to come up and that it's not directed at them personally. When I was feeling so terrible during those early weeks, some of this undirected stuff got directed at Jim simply because he was there."

## Unrealistic Expectations

In trying to understand what your wife is experiencing during the first 10 or 12 weeks of pregnancy, consider, first, the actual physical changes and the fact that there are numerous ways in which her body can react to them. In addition, remember other important factors that may affect her reactions—how she feels about you, how she feels about her own parents, how she feels about becoming a mother, how she feels about the economic situation you are both in. She faces the same questions you face during pregnancy, but there is more pressure on her, because she is bearing a child in a society that has incredibly high expectations of mothers. "We believe we're superbeings," said nurse and childbirth educator Janet Barnett at the 1979 conference of the International Childbirth Education Association in New Orleans. Barnett, an expert in family-centered maternity care, was arguing for maternity care that supports families, so that mothers will not have to bear all the responsibilities, so they will not have to be all things to their husbands and to their families. Margot Edwards, a California childbirth educator, said, "Women have too many expectations of themselves."

If a woman's expectations are too high, she may be susceptible to being too quickly discouraged during pregnancy, especially at the beginning. A few months after she became pregnant, twenty-one-year-old Lynne volunteered to babysit for her sister-in-law's two-month-old infant. The baby, unable to burp after she fed him, was extremely cranky and inconsolable. "All I could think of," said Lynne, "was this poor little kid who had to burp. He was crying and crying. Nothing would make him happy. I was losing my temper fast. When I got home later on, I went to bed and began crying. I said to Skip, 'It's going to be awful. I couldn't even take care of this poor little kid and I lost my temper so fast.' Then I thought, 'What have I got myself into? Did I really make a big mistake?' Later I felt horrible about having second thoughts." Not realizing that women don't have magical powers in caring for children—they have to learn how to care for them and it takes time and patience—Lynne thought she could be instantly successful in caring for an infant. Her expectations were so high that she felt like a failure when she couldn't console an infant. Luckily, her husband, who had grown up in a large family and was an uncle to sixteen nephews and nieces, was much more experienced with infants than she was. Because of his experience, he was able to offer Lynne much needed support at a time when she was suffering from too high expectations and the second thoughts that follow them.

Commenting on some of the challenges with which she had to deal when she became pregnant, Laura, whose situation was generally similar to Lynne's, said, "One of my problems was expectations. I had too high expectations for myself. It would have helped if I had realized it was only a season of my life that would soon pass, then I could have been more relaxed."

*Your* expectations of your wife may be another factor that could affect how your wife feels during early pregnancy. If your expectations are too high and you find it difficult to accept that she's behaving differently because of pregnancy, you may make matters worse. In addition to handling some of the natural physical challenges of early pregnancy, she now has to fret over your feelings, how you are faring, and how to make things better for you. Said Elizabeth, whose husband had an extremely difficult time understanding what she was going through during pregnancy, "I think husbands shouldn't have such high expectations of their wives, expecting them to continue doing everything like cooking, cleaning, taking care of the children, being a fully active sex partner, all while working full time." Elizabeth and her husband came close to getting divorced after their first child was born, but managed to work out their differences with the help of a counseling psychologist. Her husband eventually learned to lower his expectations and share the responsibilities of child rearing and maintaining a house. At the same time, Elizabeth stopped trying to be a superwoman.

## Feelings about Motherhood

How your wife feels about becoming a mother also strongly affects her initial responses to being pregnant. She may be quite enthusiastic, while at the same time having doubts and fears. These negative feelings add to the pressures presented by the physical changes and can contribute to her feeling bad. Said Elizabeth about the first weeks of her pregnancy, "We planned to have a child and I was glad I was pregnant, but I was also worried as to whether I had made the right decision. I was feeling sick all the time and I was exhausted. Feeling sick doesn't make you feel glad about being a mother right away." Lynne, who also felt sick frequently during the early weeks of her pregnancy, said, "I was thrilled when I first became pregnant. Then I was worried, more worried than thrilled after a while. I was worried about whether or not we were going to be able to afford it. It was a big worry because we had just gotten married. We weren't even on our feet, and we had just bought this house. I wasn't even settled into being a wife yet, never mind turning into a mother."

Once a woman enters into the second trimester, her body has successfully made the major adjustments to being pregnant and generally she feels very good. She begins to gain weight more quickly and starts looking more and more pregnant. During the last part of the fourth month or during the fifth month, between the eighteenth and twentieth weeks, any tension of the first trimester is overshadowed by the dramatic event that now begins. At this time, the pregnant woman starts feeling the baby's movements. This quickening means that for your wife—and for you—the baby is no longer just a growing bundle of possibilities but is a more "visible" and tangible reality, a being who tosses and turns and stretches his arms and kicks his feet. At first, all this movement is very gentle because the fetus at four or five months still weighs only a little over 1/2 pound. But your wife feels it, nevertheless, and this may change things considerably for her. If she's had lingering doubts about her pregnancy, about becoming a mother, the baby's movements may make her more at ease and make her feel more excited about him.

"I first felt my baby," said Elizabeth, who is a teacher and an artist, "when I was about four and a half months pregnant. It felt like someone was doing a painting inside my stomach using staccato brush strokes like an impressionist painter. I began feeling very close to the baby. The bigger he got, the more I realized I had a human being within me." Another mother said, "The first feeling I had was like a rippling movement, a kind of stretching of my stomach muscles. Although I was in love with her from the first moment I knew she existed, she became more real to me between the fourth and fifth months, when I could feel her move and then when I heard her heartbeat for the first time. I loved her enormously. I felt grateful and excited and very tender. I felt extremely protective."

## Your Wife's Concerns—and Yours

Even if a woman's feelings toward the baby and about the pregnancy in general are very positive, she still may have pressing fears about the baby and may, from time to time, feel down in the dumps. Said one expectant mother, "I was worried what the baby was going to be like, whether he'd have all his fingers and toes, whether I'd have a miscarriage, and whether I would be a good mother." If your wife has similar concerns, they may pose an extra challenge. It may be harder for you to deal with her worries and concerns now that she's feeling so well physically and is still the focus of so much attention, especially as she begins to grow bigger and rounder. It's sometimes easier to offer support and understanding to someone whose physical symptoms are evident. When someone's fears and worries are not accompanied by physical symptoms, it is harder to empathize, especially if you've never been faced with a similar situation. In fact, you may feel left out and think that your worries and concerns are being ignored. Said one expectant father whose wife was six months pregnant, "We had gone to a party with some of our friends and, as usual, everyone was fussing over Peggy. But one of our friends made it a point to come over to me and ask me how I was doing. She was genuinely interested. I was surprised. It was delightful to receive a little attention."

The feelings you and your wife are experiencing are complex. Both of you are making a major transition that is exciting, intricate, and difficult. If you talk openly and frequently to each other about your feelings, you may avoid unnecessary conflicts and better enjoy the excitement of becoming parents. Laura had many fears about her pregnancy during the first three months but not as many after that. But Laura's husband, too, had a great many fears. "He let me talk about my feelings," said Laura, "and he was an enormous support, but he wouldn't talk about his feelings. He was afraid the baby would be deformed or retarded. He never mentioned these fears to me till afterwards, till after Cindy was born. It would have been better if he could have told me his fears. If he had, I could have reassured him." It's good to remember that you may also need reassurance from time to time. If you and your wife communicate freely with one another, you will be better able to offer her support when she needs it and to receive reassurance when you need it.

## Size and Self-Image

As the pregnancy progresses and a woman grows larger, she may become uncomfortable because of her size. The baby is now growing rapidly and the uterus is expanding. This causes added pressure on the woman's diaphragm, and she may experience shortness of breath. Added pressure on her lower abdomenal region may cause her to urinate more frequently and to have difficulty with her bowel movements. A more pressing concern to her, however, may be her feelings about her self-image now that she has gained 15, 20, or 25 pounds. Our society places much importance on having a thin and shapely figure, and a woman may feel upset about her new, larger shape. This weight gain is temporary, but to a woman pregnant for the first time the extra pounds may seem hopelessly permanent. One mother, who was very sensitive during pregnancy to her new weight gain, told how years before it had taken her a great deal of effort and will power to be thin, and that she was upset now about having to gain so much extra weight. "When I was in high school," she explained, "I was fat. After high school I worked hard at losing weight. Now I was fat again and I didn't want my husband to see me this way. I didn't want him to touch me because I was so fat. I wanted to keep hiding by body under the covers." Said another mother, "By the last month, I had gained 25 pounds. I was downright fat. I didn't like all this weight because it was difficult to get around. Besides, it was July and very hot, which made me feel even worse. I was sick of being pregnant, of waiting and waiting and being so huge."

Once again, if you are empathetic and can provide an atmosphere where your wife can talk about her feelings, she'll feel better. Frank and open discussions of her feelings and your feelings may bring about a refreshing reevaluation of some deep-seated and confining notions of what beauty is and what it means to be pregnant. One expectant father, whose wife used to get upset frequently over her added poundage, said he helped his wife a lot by constantly reassuring her about how beautiful she really was. "I would kid her as well," he said. "I'd say, 'Joan you have now reached the point where you look better with your clothes on than with them off.'" Many women may be offended at such humor, but Padraic's wife appreciated the good intentions behind it. His show of affection coupled with his sense of humor worked effectively.

## Open Communication

One of the major challenges for you and your wife as pregnancy progresses is the gradual change that takes place regarding your relationship to each other. A third person, both "visible" and silent for the time being, is emerging and changing the way each of you thinks about yourself and relates to the other. If, as one mother expressed it, the lines of communication aren't kept open, the birth of a child can cause overwhelming challenges to a relationship, a factor sometimes overlooked by expectant parents. One father said, "Our relationship during pregnancy was terrible. She was sick all of the time." His wife explained, "The last few months of my pregnancy, we didn't really communicate. Because I felt rotten all the time, I never wanted to snuggle with him. I'd say, 'Leave me alone; I want to go to sleep.' I blamed him for making me feel so rotten. I told him it was his fault. He'd go to work, I'd see him and say 'Hi, how are you?' 'How's supper?'—'Good.' 'Want any breakfast?'—'No.' We didn't communicate because I was a different person almost. I wasn't normal. I was different from him now. Before, we were together, now I was by myself. It felt like I was put over here away from him and I was going to be there for nine months. Toward the very end I wanted to get back." Because of the enormous emotional changes your wife and you experience, breakdowns in communication can easily occur.

If the lines of communication are open, however, the period of pregnancy and birth brings with it the opportunity for enormous personal growth. A man and a woman actually draw closer in their relationship to each other, since the positive aspects of their experience outweigh the negative. According to University of Houston psychologist Dr. John Vincent, the period of pregnancy and birth is a time when new parents become full-fledged adults. "They gain confidence in their ability to deal with stress and rise above unpleasant circumstances and win," says Dr. Vincent. "This sense of accomplishment, this sense of family continuity, has real positive effects on them." The positive effects come about because each partner has to come to grips with developing a greater sensitivity to the major changes both are experiencing. Says Dr. Philip Cowan, a University of California-Berkeley psychologist, "Like being in a new territory, it's a new opportunity to take a look at yourself, to reorganize, to start communicating in a different way, to make more use of the time you have." The struggle is made easier if the positive is stressed over the negative.

As your child continues to develop in the womb, if you and your wife are open with one another about your feelings, you actually will grow closer to each other and set a pattern of communication that lays the groundwork for a fruitful, supportive relationship between you and your wife and between each of you and your child. Said one mother, "It was a struggle for us, but when we both realized that we were having the baby *together*, we became much closer."

Finally, there is the subject of sex. This part of a relationship is always a sensitive, private, and emotional one. Because of the added pressures of pregnancy, sexual relations are the ones that often suffer most. Pregnancy may require a change in the frequency of sexual activity, as well as different approaches and greater sensitivity to each others' needs. We will now turn to a discussion of this private issue, and see it in the context of pregnancy and childbirth.

# 4

# Sex and Pregnancy

# Sex during Pregnancy: The Challenges

Making love during pregnancy can be one of the most difficult challenges and one of the most pleasant and tender experiences of pregnancy. How you face sexuality may establish a pattern that will bring you and your wife closer together or draw you, ultimately, further and further apart.

One of the major challenges of sex during pregnancy has nothing to do with the condition of pregnancy *per se* but with how you may view and understand sex itself. Consider the situation of Jennifer and Todd and their experience during Jennifer's pregnancy. Regarding sex during the first three months of her pregnancy, Jennifer said, "I was very sick, and sexually, as far as that goes, I didn't want him to touch me. For quite some time I had to become an actress when it came to sexual activity. It was like I was being raped. I resented it. I was angry. I didn't have any feeling for it. I was upset. I just couldn't stand it." Jennifer's husband tried to understand what was happening to her, but it was difficult for him. "I tried to be understanding," he said, "but for those first couple of months, when Jennifer first became pregnant, she would come home after work in the evening and just about die. She was sick and she was tired. She'd go upstairs and lie down on the bed, and I'd lie down with her. I used to say, 'If this is going to keep up for nine months, I just can't stand it.' " Sensing Todd's frustration, Jennifer reluctantly made love with him.

The first three months of her pregnancy posed great difficulty for Jennifer because of all the hormonal, physical, and psychological changes she was facing. In addition, her full-time job left her very tired. Given all these factors, it is understandable that she did not want to engage in sexual activity with her husband. But the tension brought about by the changes and Jennifer's fatigue actually concealed some deeper issues that she and Todd needed to confront. Note how Jennifer described her experience: "sexually, as far as that goes," "I resented it," and "I just couldn't stand it." "That" and "it" are used to refer to sex with her husband. She reduces "sex" to intercourse, disassociating it from her feelings. For Jennifer, sex also meant satisfying Todd's needs at her expense. Said Jennifer, "After the pregnancy, I gained a greater sense of what sex means to him. It doesn't affect me nearly as much. When he brings up the subject, it's like 'Shall we go out to dinner this weekend.' I don't physically feel anything and he does. I don't understand it." Asked about his wife's response to his demands, Todd said, "It did affect me, but it didn't seem to me like it was an imposition; it wasn't like she was refusing me. It wasn't the same thing like 'Oh, no! not tonight, I've got a headache.' I turned my activities to something else. I just had to get my mind on something, to try to be understanding of the situation."

Todd also equated sex with intercourse and talked about his acceptance of temporarily not having this need met. What both he and Jennifer experienced was the classic challenge of sexual relations—expressing one's feelings through giving pleasure and receiving pleasure while also respecting each other as persons. Put simply, the challenge for each person is neither to be a slave, dominated by your partner, nor to be a tyrant dominating your partner. On the one hand, Jennifer deceived her husband by acting as if she were enjoying making love with him, an action that made her subservient to his desires. She resented this dishonesty and was depressed by it. On the other hand, whether Todd was oblivious to Jennifer's feelings or just ignored them, his behavior was a form of tyranny or dominance. The problem they faced existed before Jennifer became pregnant. Pregnancy exacerbated the problem because of the numerous pressures both Jennifer and Todd were facing. Being pregnant posed a threat to their relationship, but also gave them the opportunity to deal with this threat and resolve some difficulties in how they were relating to each other. Jennifer and Todd's experience was not an uncommon one for expectant fathers and mothers.

Jennifer and Todd still haven't resolved all of the major conflicts that their sexual experience during pregnancy exposed, but they have made one major step in resolving some of them. After several months of faking, of pretending she was enjoying making love with Todd, Jennifer quit acting. She said, "It finally got to the point where I said 'I can't stand it any more. I'll tell Todd how I feel.' " To her amazement, Todd took it well. "He was very gentle. He understood how I felt. He relaxed and then I became relaxed about it." When Jennifer stopped pretending and told Todd how she really felt, Todd reciprocated. They began to be more honest with each other, an important factor not just related to sexual activity during pregnancy but to every aspect of a love relationship. When they did resume making love again after the initial weeks of pregnancy, it was in a more honest and relaxed atmosphere. "When it became comfortable for me again," said Jennifer, "it was exciting and we were very close."

To turn the challenges you may encounter regarding sex and pregnancy into opportunities to express your love and affection, consider the following discussion of these major points:

*Sex during pregnancy is normal, healthy, and needed.*
*Expectant mothers and fathers each respond differently to the experience of sex during pregnancy.*

## Sex during Pregnancy: Normal, Healthy, Needed

Until recently, intercourse during pregnancy was almost a taboo. Many obstetrician-gynecologists discouraged expectant mothers from having sex during the first ten weeks or so of pregnancy and during the last six to eight weeks for fear of interfering with the pregnancy and harming the developing baby. Other than their direct recommendations of abstention, doctors often totally avoided discussing the subject of sex during pregnancy, thus leaving their patients without adequate information and encouragement. Largely as a result of the childbirth education movement and the current open atmosphere regarding sex, doctors are generally much more understanding and open in dealing with sex during pregnancy. Unless there is some medically sound reason for your wife to avoid intercourse during pregnancy, such as a history of miscarriages, her doctor will encourage her to continue her normal sexual behavior and answer any questions she may have. As a matter of fact, many doctors prefer that you accompany your wife from time to time during her regular prenatal checkups. If you and your wife have any questions or concerns about making love during pregnancy, raise them together. If both of you receive clear explanations from the doctor, this may help you avoid any misunderstandings that could arise if you weren't present to ask your own questions.

Now that the atmosphere regarding sex during pregnancy is more supportive, there are other problems to contend with. One problem is the danger of going to a new extreme: According to one childbirth educator, now that sex is permitted and encouraged during pregnancy, expectant mothers are being pressured into behaving as if pregnancy should make no difference in their sexual relations with their husbands. At the 1979 conference of the International Childbirth Education Association in New Orleans, Margot Edwards, a childbirth educator, complained about the problem expectant mothers face as a result of the general acceptance of sex during pregnancy. Said Edwards, "We say to expectant mothers it's now okay to have intercourse, but the problem is that they are asked to be too much. We give them permission to do these things and ask too much of them." In other words, the condition of pregnancy and how it may affect women emotionally is ignored.

Women are thus expected to be superbeings and ignore the emotional, physical, and hormonal changes they undergo. It's as if sex were solely a matter of will and not a complex reality involving one's entire being. By ignoring all the other factors affecting a person's sexual responses, sex becomes a less than human experience.

Heightened and unrealistic expectations are related to a more fundamental problem: equating sex with intercourse. In such an equation, the only thing that seems to matter is that now expectant fathers can have intercourse with their wives and all they need to know is what is the most comfortable position for their wives and how can they avoid hurting the baby. Unfortunately, by focusing on actions, what one can or cannot do, how one can do it, when to and when not to do it, it is easy to overlook the deep feelings, the meaning, the joy, the tenderness, and the mystery that expectant parents can communicate to each other in their sexual relations. Complained one mother, "My husband was frustrated that we couldn't carry on making love as we did before. He was constantly interested in reading about different positions to use in making love during pregnancy and then trying them out. But nothing happened because it was too difficult to try them out, especially near the end, because I was too fat and uncomfortable. I don't think sexual relations always have to be intercourse. I think my husband came to this realization—that women weren't mechanical, that all you do is turn on the engine and rev it up and off it goes. I think it was painful for him but he had no other choice." Her husband reluctantly agreed with her assessment. "I was programmed, like lots of men, to look at sex in a restrictive way," he said. "Sex always meant having intercourse, so it was hard when Elizabeth was always feeling so lousy. It was hard to learn there are also other ways of expressing your sexual feelings."

Elisabeth Bing, coauthor with Libby Colman of *Making Love During Pregnancy,* tells the expectant mothers in her classes that they can live an ordinary life and do what they like, unless their doctors prohibit them from doing something. Regarding sex and pregnancy, she encourages them to continue making love, unless otherwise instructed by their doctor. "You have to find many different ways of making love," she told one of her recent childbirth classes. "It's a reaffirmation of the love of a man and woman. It's a demonstration of care and support. During pregnancy, often a woman's self-esteem suffers. Making love is good because it builds self-esteem and because it's pleasurable."

But making love does not necessarily mean having intercourse. It could take the form of caressing, embracing, touching, massaging. "Women don't always want to have intercourse," said Margot Edwards, "but they do want to be shown other forms of affection like touching or massaging." Many childbirth educators and psychologists contend that expectant mothers especially need such demonstrations of affection during pregnancy because they are at this time more vulnerable and sensitive as a result of the changes they are undergoing.

But what about an expectant father? He is also encountering many changes during the pregnancy period and sexual relations with his wife are important. Often he is neglected while his wife receives most of the attention. His wife may be so preoccupied with preparing for the baby that she ignores his need for physical affection and concern. One mother, who believes husbands shouldn't feel neglected just because their wives are preoccupied with the changes associated with pregnancy, said, "On the other hand, I think wives shouldn't be overdemanding. They should be considerate of their husbands' feelings." A woman's being sensitive to her husband's need for affection can express her feelings through sexual intercourse or by embracing, caressing, massaging, or by genital stimulation orally or by hand, which culminates in orgasm. As with sexual relations during any period of one's life, expectant fathers and mothers must mutually work out a harmonious balance between expressing affection sexually and receiving it.

## Expectant Mothers and Fathers: Different Responses to Sex

Not affected adversely by any hormonal changes during pregnancy, some women continue the same level of sexual activity they always have had. Others may be mildly affected, usually during the first three months, and may show a decreased desire. Some women are so strongly affected by pregnancy that they have very little interest or desire throughout the entire nine months. As with other aspects of life, a woman's feelings about sex during pregnancy depend on a host of conditions and circumstances: her feelings about being pregnant, her attitude toward sex, her feelings about you, her emotional and physical reactions to the hormonal changes, her feelings about her enlarged shape, her feelings about becoming a mother, her energy level, and her fears that intercourse may harm the baby.

Although sex and pregnancy are no longer considered incompatible, until recently there's been very little research on the subject. Several recent major studies, however, including one by Dr. William Masters and Virginia Johnson, have shown that there is a steady pattern regarding a pregnant woman's desire for sex during pregnancy. During the first trimester, when a woman experiences the most radical changes of pregnancy, she has a decrease in desire. In the second trimester, there is an increase in desire, and during the third trimester, there is gradual decrease in desire as the day of delivery approaches. Other studies, done in the United States and in Europe, including one by researchers at the University of Washington in Seattle, discovered a slightly different trend.* Most pregnant women, according to these studies, experienced a steady decrease both in desire for and involvement in all aspects of sexuality throughout pregnancy. In the University of Washington study most of the 260 women had not been adequately informed by their doctors about alternatives to coitus or about other positions that may have been more suitable. The decline in interest and activity, it is implied, may be due to lack of proper information and encouragement.

Although the research that exists about women and sexual desire and activity during pregnancy is inconclusive and sketchy at best, one conclusion is clear: How a woman responds to sex during pregnancy is a complex and individual matter. Expectant fathers, therefore, should keep this in mind, aware of the need to be extremely sensitive to their wives' feelings.

Here are a few examples of how some expectant mothers and fathers felt about the experience of sex during pregnancy and how they dealt with the experience.

Laura had had two previous miscarriages and was instructed by her doctor to abstain from intercourse at least during the first three months, as, in his opinion, during this period she would be most susceptible to having a miscarriage. In Laura's situation, her doctor didn't have to advise her against having intercourse because she never felt well enough anyway during the first trimester. "We couldn't have sex for the first three or four months," recounted Laura. "I had had two miscarriages and was afraid of having another one. Besides, I was awfully nervous and anxious."

During those early months, Laura suffered from insomnia and was literally seized by fear. But at the start of the second trimester, she reacted very much like the majority of women who have some difficulties in the early stages of pregnancy. She started to feel terrific. Buoyed by the knowledge

*Don A. Solberg, Julius Butler, M.D., and Nathaniel N. Wagner, Ph.D., "Sexual Behavior during Pregnancy," **New England Journal of Medicine**, May 24, 1973, pages 1098–1103.

that the danger period was over, she started to relax and resume having sexual relations with her husband. "Once I was past that first stage," recalled Laura, "I had no fear at all and was sure that everything was going to turn out well. We began having sex again and I thought it was exciting." Not only was it exciting for her but the entire nature of sexual activity took on a new meaning. Laura continued, "I was always a raucous and playful sexual partner, but during pregnancy, I became more sensual, more calm, warm, and smooth—not as raucous and playful. I also used to enjoy x-rated films and dirty jokes but I didn't like them anymore. Sex became sacred to me because I was feeling the enormity of what was going on inside my body. I couldn't separate that from sexual contact. Sex became even more positive for me."

Many expectant fathers undergo similar changes in outlook regarding sex. One example is Mark, who spent much of the first trimester of his wife's pregnancy sexually frustrated. They had been married only a few months when they discovered that Robin was pregnant, and suddenly Mark felt he was alone. Robin's discomfort and her lack of interest in making love made Mark irritable. He didn't handle his frustration well and frequently argued with Robin over embarassingly minor matters. He was insensitive to Robin's feelings and sometimes ridiculed her. "We fought a lot," said Mark, "over the pettiest things. I was under a lot of pressure at work and then when I came home at night I always had to be so giving and understanding. I couldn't stand it." Mark's arguing and failure to empathize made Robin more and more unresponsive to him. The ensuing vicious cycle of resentment and miscommunication continued for a few months until Mark and Robin finally resolved their problem through long and painful discussions about the changes each was going through. Such openness is the basis for any healthy sexual relationship. For Mark, this openness was hard but it led him to change, especially regarding his understanding of sex. Once Robin felt better and they had resolved their initial conflicts, they resumed making love as they had before. "At first," said Mark, "sex was not substantially different than it was before. But later I noticed I had changed." Late in Robin's pregnancy, she grew quite uncomfortable because of all her added weight and she experienced difficulty making love. She also suffered a loss of self-esteem. Said Mark, "She felt ugly because she was so fat. She looked at herself in the mirror and thought she was ugly." Mark countered Robin by telling her how he felt about her, that he thought she was beautiful. He expressed how he felt sexually toward Robin in tender ways other than intercourse. This represented a major change for him. "For me," said Mark, "it was an expansion of my concept of sexuality. I didn't feel frustrated as I was before, and this led me to believe I had reached another level of sexuality, through other ways of communicating my feelings."

More complex than one is first led to believe, sex and pregnancy pose challenges that may at times take a few years to meet successfully. If a man and a woman had a good sexual relationship, and in addition are open with one another regarding their feelings about sex, they will continue to have a good sexual experience throughout pregnancy, no matter what obstacles they have to face. "We had a good sexual relationship," remarked John, a father who said he and his wife had to refrain from having intercourse only during the last few weeks. But this didn't affect them much, explained John. In fact their sexual relationship improved. "Being attentive to each other was just as important as making love. We don't always have to have intercourse. I've always known this, but Karen's pregnancy just made it easier to be open about this fact."

If a man and a woman aren't open with each other about their feelings regarding sex during pregnancy, they may survive the pregnancy but a pattern of poor communication can develop that, if not resolved, can draw them further and further apart. This was the experience of Michael and his wife Brenda. When Brenda became pregnant, she felt tired frequently and had her share of morning sickness. But even though during the first twelve weeks of pregnancy she was not too keen about making love, she made love to Michael fairly regularly. "I think we made love so much," said Michael, "because I was so demanding. I'm afraid I wasn't as sympathetic as I could have been to how she felt. But she didn't refuse me either." During the second trimester, Brenda felt better and enjoyed making love. "When I wasn't overtired," said Brenda, "I enjoyed it. It was relaxing." But during the four or five weeks before the birth she was more tired from carrying around an extra 25 pounds and felt too uncomfortable to have intercourse. She was reluctant to refuse him, however, so they continued having sexual intercourse. They actually had intercourse 24 hours before the baby was born. "I used to boast about this," said Michael, "but now I don't because I think I was very insensitive to Brenda's feelings. I was so overbearing and Brenda just refused to say no."

In the months after the baby was born, their relationship deteriorated. Brenda had all the responsibilities of taking care of their child, which she resented. This resentment spilled over into their sexual relationship and when Brenda wasn't feeling up to making love, she started saying no to Michael. "Having sex after the baby was born," recalled Michael, "was difficult. It was like you had to make an appointment." Finally after a year of suffering a deteriorating relationship, Brenda and Michael sought the help of a counselling psychologist, and through a long, difficult year of trying to come to grips with their feelings, resentments, and how they related to each other, they fortunately were able to reestablish a stronger relationship. As a reflection of this, their sexual relationship improved dramatically. Three years later, they decided to have another child. When Brenda got pregnant again, she and Michael had a much more open and relaxed sexual relationship. "When Brenda was pregnant the second time," said Michael, "we didn't make love nearly as much because she was tired so often. I still didn't like the infrequency, but I was much more patient and when we did make love, it was beautiful. We related to each other better. We were closer than ever before. I was much more sensitive to Brenda's feelings and I think she was much more honest about hers."

## Postpartum Considerations

It should be noted that what applies to your sexual relationship with your wife during pregnancy also applies after the baby is born, especially during the postpartum period, which lasts up to six weeks. During this period, though your wife may feel generally very healthy she may be exhausted nevertheless. Her exhaustion is due to the strain of giving birth, and it is difficult for her to regain her strength quickly because of the demands of her new schedule. Newborn babies, even quiet cooperative ones, need time to adjust to life outside the womb and, as a result, will demand a great deal of attention day and night.

Meeting the baby's needs for warmth, food, love, and cuddling, while a woman's body is recovering from the birth will affect her sexual desire and her ability to resume sexual relations right away. She still may be overweight and feel discouraged because of this. If she's had an episiotomy or a vaginal tear, it may take six weeks or longer for it to heal and for her to feel comfortable having intercourse again. In addition, she may be impatient that this recovery process takes so long. Said Janet Barnett, a nurse and childbirth educator, "We believe we're superbeings and can get off the delivery table and resume normal functions immediately."

Another physical consideration is that a woman's breasts, which have become fuller and heavier in later pregnancy, will be particularly sensitive during a few days after the birth because they are producing colostrum, a yellowish fluid that acts as a laxative for the breast-fed baby. Mother's milk usually begins flowing by the fourth or fifth day. If your wife breast-feeds the baby, her breasts will remain especially sensitive, particularly during the early weeks. To nurse successfully, she should be relaxed and confident; if she's not, her milk supply is diminished, which in turn may upset the baby. It is important at this time that you offer her the support and understanding she needs to nurse the baby comfortably and successfully. Once the adjustment period of the early weeks is over, remember that your wife's breasts will continue to be more sensitive than normal. They are so responsive to touch, for example, that they will easily and freely express milk, a reality that you should be aware of, especially after you resume making love.

All the factors mentioned above may affect how long it takes a woman to feel physically fit again after the birth. This, of course, affects how she feels about sexual relations. You, too, may feel various pressures during this period. If you're helping to care for the baby, you also may be exhausted from interrupted sleep and you may be struggling with adjusting to a new time schedule—or lack of one—as a result of the baby's presence. As you did during your wife's pregnancy, you will have to exercise patience and a great deal of understanding. Before you can resume having sexual intercourse again, both you and your wife will have to express your sexual feelings in other ways, careful always to respect not only each other's feelings, but the postpartum tenderness of your wife's body. If you've grown closer to your wife during pregnancy, making some more adjustments in expressing your love and affection for her will be easier.

# Sex During Pregnancy: Suggestions and Comments

### Understanding
Respect your wife's feelings no matter how difficult it may be at times. If you are upset and baffled by what she's experiencing, especially during early pregnancy, and act insensitively, your wife will become more and more unresponsive. Thus a vicious cycle will ensue and poor sexual relations will be only one of many resulting problems. A good sexual relationship is built on mutual respect, caring, and open and honest communication. How you handle the tensions in your sexual relationship during pregnancy will set the tone for later.

### Fears
Don't overlook your fears and those of your wife. First, get your questions and concerns out in the open. Will having intercourse cause a miscarriage? Will it harm the baby? Late during the pregnancy, will intercourse cause premature birth? Address your questions to your wife's obstetrician-gynecologist and don't be bashful. Follow his or her advice. In general, sex during pregnancy is not only encouraged but safe and beneficial to both you and your wife. There are some exceptions, and your wife's doctor should inform you if intercourse should be avoided during pregnancy and during what periods. If it should, remember there are innumerable ways of expressing your physical affection for your wife as well as receiving physical satisfaction. Expectant parents should be encouraged to continue making love unless otherwise instructed by their doctor. "You have many different ways of making love," said Elisabeth Bing. "Many doctors say you should stop making love only when you go into labor." Although some research has demonstrated that coitus does not bring about complications during late pregnancy, doctors highly recommend that intercourse then be engaged in with great tenderness. A husband should be careful to enter his wife with gentle, shallow thrusts so as not to aggravate the vaginal and cervical tissues, which then are very soft. If your wife has any bleeding or any unusual discomfort after intercourse, do not continue having intercourse and have your wife immediately consult with her doctor.

### Positions
Although many men and women are concerned that the male dominant position may be harmful to the baby, it is an unfounded concern. It may be an uncomfortable position for you, however, because it's hard making love while supporting yourself in a push-up position. And it may be uncomfort-

able for your wife due to all the extra weight. Actually, both of you may find other positions more comfortable and a welcome variety both during and after pregnancy. The female dominant position is a position preferred by many women during pregnancy. It puts less pressure on their bodies and they have better control over how deeply the penis will penetrate. Another position is side-to-side: You and your wife face each other, a position that frees her from any undue pressure. Another position involves your being at your wife's back, entering her vagina from behind. Until late pregnancy, these and other positions will give you enough variety so that both you and your wife will be comfortable—and comfort should be a main concern. Toward the end of pregnancy, make sure that while making love you do so with gentle, shallow thrusts.

## Medical Considerations

If you have any questions or concerns about what you can and cannot do sexually and how it will affect the pregnancy, always consult your doctor. For example, there are some situations during the course of pregnancy in which a woman must abstain from having orgasms whether as a result of intercourse or through manual stimulation. And there are some, although very few, situations where oral-genital sex (cunnilingus) can bring about a herpes infection.

There are two things you should be aware of regarding physiological changes your wife experiences that may affect sex during pregnancy. One is the vaginal discharge that occurs during pregnancy. The other is how your wife experiences an orgasm—especially in the later stages of pregnancy. You should be aware of these two areas of change because they may affect your feelings about your sexual activity.

In most instances, cunnilingus during pregnancy is acceptable and safe. It can be, along with fellatio, a welcome alternative to intercourse at various times throughout pregnancy. You should be aware, if you haven't discovered this already, that there are increased amounts of vaginal discharge resulting from the pregnancy and, of course, from any sexual stimulation. Although perfectly natural and normal, the discharge may have a different odor and taste, one which may or may not affect your feelings about oral-genital sex. Some doctors recommend that if this causes either you or your wife any discomfort, you could use a scented oil. To be aware of this change and your feelings about it will help you handle it sensitively and intelligently.

The other physiological change you should be aware of deals with the nature of your wife's experience of orgasm during pregnancy, especially during the last trimester. According to Masters and Johnson, there is a four-phase sexual response cycle: First, a stage of arousal or excitement, the time one experiences gradually being sexually aroused; second, a plateau stage, a period of steady heightened excitement prior to orgasm; third, orgasm itself; and fourth, resolution, a period of transition from sexual excitement to a more quiescent state. During the excitement phase, blood rushes to the vaginal area, resulting in an increased sensitivity to the pleasures of sexual activity. Ordinarily, the rush of blood, which reaches a peak during orgasm, abates after orgasm as the body returns to a quieter state. But if a woman is pregnant, especially toward the later stages of pregnancy, there is already an added supply of blood in the region of the vagina. So, when she has an orgasm during this third phase of sexual response, the area is also so engorged with blood that she experiences a much slower resolution or release. In other words, coming down is slower, and she may experience tension for a longer period of time. It just takes longer for the added blood to return and for the muscles to relax. Orgasm usually causes the uterus to contract, an integral part of the experience of sexual enjoyment, but in late pregnancy, the contractions are stronger, last a bit longer because of the slowness of the resolution phase, and can cause your wife some concern. Elisabeth Bing noted that, "When a woman has an orgasm during pregnancy, she will come down slower. She may feel her uterus contract more but she shouldn't worry about this." Of course, if your wife experiences bleeding after intercourse or any other symptoms that concern her, she should consult her doctor immediately.

As the topics touched on in this chapter show, sex during pregnancy presents extra challenges to both you and your wife. But in the long run, these challenges can bring both of you closer to each other and add a deeper dimension to how you express yourselves sexually.

# The Costs of Having a Baby

Lynne and Skip were married less than a year. They had not talked much about having a child. It was understood that they both very much wanted to be parents. When Lynne found out she was pregnant, she rushed out, bought a T-shirt with the word "Daddy" emblazoned across the front, and presented it to Skip during a surprise visit at Skip's office. Skip was excited but shocked. "My biggest fear," said Skip, "was money. Could we afford to dress him?" Skip was disturbed that this was his major concern at the time of first learning he was to become a father. "Money," he said, "It's a terrible society we live in when we're so preoccupied with money!" "It was a big worry," added Lynne, "especially because we had only recently gotten married. We weren't even on our feet, and we had just bought a house." Skip's concern about money, about the costs of having and raising a child, is a universal concern, especially during the current difficult economic times.

Although the costs of having a child should not be "the" determining factor in whether or not you become a father, it is a factor of overall importance. To be a responsible parent, one must be able to afford a modest and comfortable existence for one's child. "Modest" and "comfortable" are relative terms, that are used here to mean food, shelter, and clothing at the plainest level. Unfortunately, many parents, even when they can't afford it, think the plainest level isn't good enough and want "nothing but the best" of material comforts for their children: new and expensive furniture, clothes, toys, etc. If you can afford the plainest regarding food, shelter, and clothing for your child, you're off to a good start. Then you can concentrate on what costs more, what sometimes is in short supply, but what is quite affordable—your love and attention and time. According to psychiatrist Robert Carr, one of the major problems he has observed in recent years is deprived children. "We see many more children who are not deprived of food or shelter but who are emotionally deprived middle-class children."

In order to be able to concentrate on being a father who, with your wife, loves and cares for your child, you should examine the costs involved in food, shelter, and clothing and make appropriate plans. If you do not set your sights too high (an infant doesn't really need new furniture, when he can sleep perfectly safely and well in a borrowed or a secondhand crib), you may be able to keep love, care, attention, and time with your child as your chief priorities.

*When you are calculating the costs of having and caring for a baby, it may help to consider the following points.*

## What Roles Will Each Parent Play in Caring for the Baby?

If your wife is currently working full time but plans to stay home with the baby for six months or for several years, her direct financial contribution to your new family is temporarily cut off. But her contribution to your child is inestimably valuable, something that often is overlooked. When Susan, a

Vermont teacher, was five months pregnant, her school term ended and she quit her job. "We decided," said Susan, "it was an ideal time for me to get ready for the baby. But I had a few more courses to take for my masters degree, so I went to school that summer. Tom had to pay for the courses and he would make offhand remarks about my not working and how expensive the courses were. He was resentful about bearing the financial burdens for both of us, now that I wasn't working." Susan and Tom's conflict over their new financial situation is not an uncommon one. If it's not dealt with out in the open and resolved, it could create unneeded tensions. So when you're considering your new financial situation, make sure that your roles are defined as clearly as possible. Furthermore, you both must understand that if your wife is going to care full time for the baby, both of you are making important contributions to the welfare of your child, and neither one should resent the other's means of contributing to this end.

## Who Will Take Care of the Baby?

If your wife returns to work three, six, nine months, or a year after the baby is born, your income level will rise again, but then you must estimate child-care costs. An important factor here is what trade-offs you are willing to make when someone else takes care of your child. In many parts of the United States and Canada, using the services of nannies is becoming increasingly popular for middle-class fathers and mothers who have active careers. The question of employing a nanny or someone in a similar position involves more than money and expertise. You must be willing to pay a substantial amount of money for a competent, capable, and loving person to care for your child, or you may wind up with inferior care, unless you're fortunate in finding a relative or neighbor who is willing to work for a low salary. It's ironic that some parents will pay the lowest wages to the person caring for their children, yet will pay large hourly fees to those who provide service for everything from lawn care to automobile repair.

## How Much Does It Cost to Have a Baby?

In 1980, the average cost of having a child in the United States, according to the Health Insurance Institute, was $1500. This figure includes a four-day hospital stay, the obstetrician's fee, labor and delivery room charges, and the pediatrician's fee for well-baby care. If a baby is born by cesarean-section, the cost is significantly higher, sometimes almost double. Because $1500 is an average figure, it's misleading. In some parts of the country it may be less, in some parts, more; and even within the same city costs will vary. In New York City in the late 1970s, the cost of a semiprivate room (with four in a room) varied from hospital to hospital by as much as $78 a day. And the cost of the nursery charge varied as much as $79 a day.

Since costs are rising rapidly and often vary so much among obstetricians and hospitals, it may pay to shop around. But don't sacrifice quality to saving money, although you may find the same quality care for a lower cost. When you are comparing prices or just estimating the total cost, consider the following categories. Space has been left for you to fill in estimated costs based on your own research.

**Obstetrician**
 *(prenatal care, delivery, and postpartum check-up)* _____

**Hospital costs**
 *Four- or five-day stay (cost per day)*
 *Semiprivate room* _____
 *Private room* _____

**Labor and delivery room** _____

**Nursery**
 *(cost per day)* _____

**Anesthesiologist**
 *(An extra fee, if necessary. Some hospitals charge this fee whether an anesthesiologist's services are required or not.)* _____

**Manner of payment**
 *(Deposits required. Policies regarding insurance company payments, etc.)* _____

**Pediatrician**
 *(Well-baby costs; cost of circumcision of a boy.)* _____

You may also want to consider alternative maternity services (see page 79). In many parts of the country there are maternity centers in hospitals that are staffed by nurse midwives whose services are substantially lower than those of physicians.

## How Far Will Your Medical Coverage Go?

*If your wife has insurance that covers maternity costs, or if you are now planning to have a child and are exploring insurance coverage, consider the following questions.*

- If your wife is employed, is she covered under a disability insurance plan? If she is, she is entitled by federal law to collect disability benefits for any time she loses from her job because of pregnancy and childbirth.
- Is there a waiting period before maternity coverage is effective? Often, a woman must be covered for five or six months before she becomes pregnant to receive full maternity coverage.
- Determine exactly what costs the insurance will cover to figure out the actual total costs you will have.
- Does the insurance company pay the doctor and hospital directly or does it reimburse you after you have paid the bills?
- If there are complications during the delivery, how much of the added costs will the insurance company pay?
- When does the insurance coverage of the baby begin? Sometimes there is a waiting period of thirty days after birth.

## What Will Basic Nursery Supplies Cost?

*Figure out the costs of such items as:*

**baby's wardrobe**

**medical supplies**

**furniture (crib, dresser, etc.)**

**carriage**

To cut down on costs, try to buy only the essential things you will need at the beginning. Remember that you will probably receive gifts for your baby, so it is sometimes better to wait to see what you will actually need, especially regarding clothes. There is certainly no need yet to buy a windup swing or other items your baby is not ready for. Remember, too, that items like cribs and high chairs last for years and years, so you can save money by buying these used or by borrowing them. Garage sales may be your best bet for getting good deals on used baby items.

## How Much Will It Cost to Raise a Child?

It is difficult to be accurate at predicting the long-range costs of raising a child. A very conservative estimate can be made based on findings from recent government and private studies. The January 1979 issue of *Parents Magazine*, for example, published a chart of annual expenses from birth through college. These annual expenses included food at home and away, clothing, housing, medical care, transportation, education, and miscellaneous expenses, and ranged from about $1600 for the first year to close to $2300 between the ages of 16 and 17. One year of college, including tuition, required fees, and room and board, ran from roughly $1700 at a two-year public institution to a little over $4500 at a private university.

It must be emphasized, however, that the figures from such studies quickly become outdated as costs continue to rise each year. In doing any long-range planning regarding costs, keep in mind that the costs remain fairly steady for the first four or five years and begin to increase gradually each year after that until the college years when they rise dramatically.

Although the costs of having a baby and raising a child seem overwhelming when you first sit down to tally up the figures, they've got to be kept in perspective. The important thing to remember is that your salary—and your wife's salary if she resumes working—will continue to increase over the years and you will be better able later to meet the additional costs that may now seem prohibitive.

# 6

# Preparing for Childbirth

Since the late 1920s and early 1930s, most births in the United States have taken place in hospitals. Previously, most women bore their children at home, often assisted by midwives. But the maternal death rate was so high that there was a shift to hospital births because hospitals were considered safer for mothers and more convenient for doctors. When women began having their children in hospitals, they placed themselves in a rigid medical environment and sacrificed much freedom for the sake of the safety and health of their newborns and themselves, and the convenience of the medical staff. They were no longer in their homes, where they were in charge, but were in an environment controlled by doctors and hospitals.

In the 1980s, most women will still be giving birth in hospitals, but things are changing for them. Largely as a result of the influential childbirth education movement during the last two decades, women now have more control over childbirth. They can make choices as to who will deliver their babies, where their babies will be born, what approach to labor and delivery they will use, and how they will spend the first minutes, hours, and days with their newborns. According to Dr. Warren Pearse, executive director of the American College of Obstetricians and Gynecologists, the choices women have demanded and now have are due to a consumer revolution. Women want to have their children in a safe environment. They are aware of all the medical assistance available to them, and are grateful for it when needed, but they want to have a major say in how their children are brought into this world.

Fathers also have been deeply affected by the consumer-oriented childbirth education movement and want to be more actively involved during pregnancy, especially during labor and delivery. It takes two persons to get pregnant and it is only fitting that the two are together to share in the experience of childbirth. Fortunately, they can be and are. In about three-quarters of the 7000 hospitals in the United States, fathers are permitted to be with their wives during the birth of their children. They are no longer ushered to hospital waiting rooms to worry and while away the time as their wives go through labor and delivery alone. Instead, they are openly welcomed by doctors and hospitals, and deeply needed and appreciated by their wives.

In order to share fully in the experience of the birth of your child, it is vitally important to remember that your wife and you are responsible for determining who will deliver your baby, where your baby will be born, and what method of delivery you will use. The choices available to you in most places across the country are numerous and exciting. Your wife's concerns have precedence over yours, because she's having the baby, but since you and she are sharing in the birth experience and you want a very active role, it is important you share, as much as you reasonably can, in the decisions regarding planning for the birth. The decisions your wife and you make, about the person who will deliver your baby, where you would like your child to be born, and which approach to birth you follow will ultimately determine how active a role you play at the birth of your child.

# Who Will Deliver Your Baby?

The single most important decision regarding childbirth is the choice of a health-care professional who is competent, experienced, open to assisting your wife and you with the kind of birth experience both of you want, and who encourages husbands to take an active role. Most women choose to be cared for by an obstetrician, although many are turning to the services of midwives. The final decision is your wife's, but it is important that you have significant input since the decision affects you as well.

## Choosing an Obstetrician

What are the obstetrician's qualifications? Find out if he is certified by the American Board of Obstetrics and Gynecology and/or is a Fellow in the American College of Obstetricians and Gynecologists. If so, you are assured he has received specialized training and is required to keep abreast of the latest developments in the field through formal education programs. By choosing such an obstetrician, you can be assured he is competent and suitably experienced.

Once you've found an obstetrician whose credentials and experience are sound and who may be recommended to you by friends as well, accompany your wife on an exploratory visit to discuss prenatal care and birth with him, to find out if you wish to use his services. Remember that you and your wife are employing his services, paying him a handsome fee, that you have a wide selection of obstetricians from which to choose, and both of you should feel absolutely comfortable with the person you finally choose.

How does he feel about natural or prepared childbirth? What approaches to childbirth are available to you? Does he encourage fathers to participate in prenatal office visits? Accompanying your wife periodically to these checkups is important because it gives you the chance to get firsthand reports on your baby's progress, to express your support for your wife, and to discuss and ask any questions you may have about the pregnancy.

How many deliveries does he perform a year? If the number is more than 400 he might be too busy to spend much time with your wife to answer all her questions during the prenatal checkups. The kind of support your wife receives during these visits is extremely important. Said one woman, "The psychological and emotional support my obstetrician gave me meant everything to us." Her obstetrician would spend as much as 20 to 25 minutes with her or with her and her husband during each visit answering questions and offering support and encouragement. If the obstetrician is in a joint practice with others and he will spend the time needed for both of you during visits, find out if he will also deliver the baby himself. If it's possible that one of his colleagues may deliver your baby, it is important to make sure the colleague agrees to your special wishes about the kind of delivery your wife and you want and the kind of role you wish to play during labor and delivery. You may want to meet him to better judge his reaction to your requests.

When does the obstetrician find it necessary to do a cesarean delivery? How often is it necessary for him to perform such deliveries? If it is necessary for your wife to have a cesarean delivery, will you be permitted to be there with her during the birth? Until recently, fathers were excluded from the delivery room if a cesarean delivery was necessary. Now more and more hospitals are allowing fathers to be present if they are adequately prepared. Lexington County Hospital in West Columbia, South Carolina, one of the most progressive hospitals in the South, has permitted fathers in the delivery room since the 1960s. In the late 1970s, the hospital began permitting fathers to attend cesarean deliveries. According to George Rentz, hospital president, the obstetricians associated with the hospital were split even in favor of and against the idea. "We tried it as a pilot project for three months," said Rentz. "If fathers were well prepared, they were permitted to attend. The project was very successful." Like hundreds of other hospitals across the country, Lexington Hospital has had many positive results with this new practice. Mothers are the chief beneficiaries because their husbands, sitting beside them (they do not actually watch the surgery), are there to offer their support and reassurance. Fathers benefit as well, because they witness the birth of their children.

Will the obstetrician support and encourage you and your wife to spend some time with your baby immediately after the birth? Will your wife be able to have skin to skin contact with the baby? Can the silver nitrate eye solution be given 45 minutes to an hour after the birth, so the baby can see around better? The first hour is extremely important for the baby, who has been in a warm, safe environment for nine months, and is suddenly exposed to the sights and sounds of the new world. This hour may be a particularly sensitive period for the baby, and for 45 minutes to an hour he may be in what some researchers call a quiet, alert state. He actually can see around him and respond to human faces. He also can turn his head in response to his mother and father's voices. For you, this hour of bonding is equally important, because it is your first exposure to your baby. It is crucial, therefore, to arrange to have some time with your newborn baby—to touch him, stroke him, cuddle him, smile at him, and talk to him. You will begin early to grow familiar with him and to feel an attachment or bond with him.

When you ask these and other questions, you might keep in mind that what you are doing is a relatively recent development. It may make you and your wife uncomfortable to realize that you have the right to choose the kind of delivery you want and that it is reasonable to be very discriminating in your choice of obstetricians. But it also may be uncomfortable for the obstetrician because he's only recently been faced with consumer demands he's never had to deal with before. Fortunately, obstetricians have steadily and gradually changed to meet the new demands of their patients. In evaluating an obstetrician's answers to your questions and concerns, the most important criteria, in addition to competence and experience, are thoughtfulness and openness. You should be able to determine quickly if he is sensitive and open to your wishes not only by what he says but by how he answers your questions. On the other hand, his expertise and experience must be respected and there may be some areas where you and your wife will have to compromise. The most important thing is for the two of you and for the obstetrician to work in an atmosphere of trust. If you can put together a birth plan, including exactly what you and your wife would like, and work out all the details of this plan with the doctor well ahead of time, you may avoid any problems or misunderstandings later.

## Choosing a Midwife

In selecting a birth attendant, you should be aware of some of the alternatives to obstetricians that exist within more traditional settings. There are two that are currently growing in popularity. The first is the certified nurse-midwife who is in joint practice with one or more obstetricians. The nurse-midwife provides prenatal care and attends the delivery of women who have routine, uncomplicated pregnancies. Many people like the combination of obstetrician and midwife because they have access to the best of both worlds. The obstetrician is medically oriented, trained and experienced in handling any medical complications should they arise, and the certified nurse-midwife is more health or wellness oriented, trained to advise and promote the normal, natural process of pregnancy and birth.

The second alternative within a more traditional setting is the certified nurse-midwives who staff birth centers within hospitals. The nurse-midwives are approved and sponsored by the hospitals, backed up by obstetricians, and offer a very thorough and important service to thousands and thousands of women. Nurse-midwives have become very popular in many regions of the country. In New York City their services are offered in over 20 hospitals. In addition to providing thorough and competent health care for expectant mothers, the nurse-midwives do so for a much lower cost than an obstetrician, a very important factor to consider when facing high hospital costs.

Certified nurse-midwives, it should be noted, are registered nurses who have done one to two years of extensive training beyond a basic nursing program. There are 24 programs in nurse-midwifery in the United States approved by the American College of Nurse-Midwives, and there are now over 2500 licensed certified nurse-midwives who are officially recognized by the American College of Obstetricians and Gynecologists.

If your wife and you decide to use the services of a certified nurse-midwife who is in practice with an obstetrician or who is at a birth center at a hospital, the questions suggested for an obstetrician would also be appropriate for her.

# Where Will Your Baby Be Born?

## Choosing a Hospital

As a result of a consumer movement regarding childbirth in the United States, more and more hospitals during recent years have changed their policies to meet the demands of a new generation of expectant mothers and fathers. Echoing the needs of these new parents, a joint task force of five major organizations of health-care providers in the late 1970s urged the development and expansion of family-centered maternity/newborn care in hospitals across the country. The five organizations included the American Academy of Pediatrics, the American College of Nurse-Midwives, the American College of Obstetricians and Gynecologists, the American Nurses' Association, and the Nurses Association of the American College of Obstetricians and Gynecologists. The task force recommended that hospitals become more family-centered so that they may provide quality health care while at the same time recognizing and adapting to the physical, social, and psychological needs of the mother, the father, and other members of their family. If you are interested in sharing the birth experience, try to arrange to use the services of a hospital or an alternative birth center in a hospital that is family-centered, a hospital whose policies and practices will bring you, your wife, your newborn child, and—if you have them—your older children closer together.

When you are considering which obstetrician or midwife to work with, find out what hospital or hospitals he or she is affiliated with and then determine if that hospital is suitable. According to one hospital administrator, "A doctor usually leads you to his choice of a hospital, and a good doctor isn't going to mess with a bad hospital." This may generally be true, but a good doctor sometimes may not have many choices regarding hospitals, so it's important that you carefully determine if the hospital he recommends is suitable. In a city where only one hospital offers family-centered maternity/newborn care, women who want this situation will choose an obstetrician only from among those who are affiliated with that hospital.

**To determine if a hospital is suitable, consider the following criteria recommended by George Rentz, President of Lexington County Hospital in West Columbia, South Carolina.**

- *Is the hospital accredited by the Joint Commission on the Accreditation of Hospitals? If it is accredited in the area of obstetrics, you can be assured it meets the minimum standards of obstetrical care.*
- *How many deliveries are done in the hospital each month? The more deliveries a hospital does, the more experience it has. To offer a major service in obstetrics, a hospital should do at least three deliveries a day or about 100 a month.*

- *Does the hospital have at least one registered nurse in the nursery at all times—24 hours a day, seven days a week?*
- *Are the obstetricians who have privileges at the hospital board-eligible (obstetricians are board-eligible for two years prior to becoming fully certified) or board-certified by the American College of Obstetricians and Gynecologists?*
- *Does the hospital have an anesthesiologist (medical doctor) on its staff to cover just that hospital? And is the anesthesiologist board-certified?*
- *Are at least 30 percent of the hospital's nursing staff registered nurses?*
- *Is your obstetrician on good terms with the hospital?*

Many of these questions can be answered by a phone call to the hospital. The administrator's office is probably the best source of information. Once you're satisfied that the hospital is competently run, it is highly recommended that you and your wife visit there and tour its obstetrical facilities. More and more hospitals invite such visits and their staff members are generally accommodating. Many childbirth education programs include hospital tours as part of the classes. If the hospital in your area does not sponsor tours, ask the hospital administrator to arrange a tour for both of you, and most likely one will be arranged. The reason many hospitals never give tours is simply that no one has ever requested them.

During a visit to the hospital, find out if its policies are family-centered. Do they allow and support fathers in playing an active part in labor and delivery? Here are some questions you may wish to ask:

- *Are you permitted to be with your wife during labor and delivery?*
- *If it is necessary for your wife to have a cesarean delivery, will you be permitted to attend?*
- *Will you be permitted to be with your wife at all times—on arrival at the hospital, while she's being prepped, during vaginal examinations? This is an important question because you will want to avoid any needless separation.*
- *Where will your wife deliver—in a labor room, a birthing room, or a delivery room?*
- *Does the hosptial prep? If so, how do its policies agree or disagree with your doctor's or midwife's policies? (For example, the doctor may not prep, but the hospital staff will insist on doing it in the doctor's absence.)*
- *If the doctor allows food or ice chips, will the hospital staff forbid them if he is not present?*
- *Does the hospital permit fathers and mothers to spend a minimum of 5 to 15 minutes with their newborn immediately after the birth?*

- *What are the hospital's policies regarding visiting hours for fathers? It's important that you have as much opportunity as possible to spend with your wife and your child during those important first days.*
- *If your wife prefers it, does the hospital permit rooming in? If so, how frequently can you visit your wife and child?*
- *What are the staff's attitudes toward breast and bottle feeding, and do they encourage both? Are breast-fed babies given formula or water between "official" feedings?*
- *Does the hospital have any programs to teach mothers and fathers how to care for their child—how to bathe, feed, and change him?*
- *What procedures does the hospital have for checking in your wife when you bring her there at the onset of labor?*

Don't forget to check on this last point. Although women who are having their first children generally have a longer labor period, occasionally signs of labor are misread and expectant mothers are taken to the hospital with only minutes to spare. You shouldn't be separated from your wife at the hospital because of checking in regulations. Your wife needs you at all times during labor, and besides, you could miss the delivery—Brian Donahue rushed his wife, Martina, to the hospital because she was in active labor. Unfortunately, he had to spend so much time downstairs registering her that he got to the delivery room too late to see his daughter born.

Talk about the registration procedure with your obstetrician or midwife and arrange for the hospital to have all the pertinent information it needs well ahead of time. If the hospital insists that someone be there to register your wife in the admitting office, then arrange for a friend to come to the hospital with you to give the necessary information.

Finally, since policies vary from hospital to hospital and in some communities you have limited choices, you should remain firm and confidently insist on what you and your wife want from your obstetrician and the hospital. If you prefer, put your plan in writing. You should be prepared, however, to make some compromises. If compromises are to be made, make them ahead of time so as to avoid any confusion at the hospital during labor and delivery and during your baby's first days.

## The Pregnant Patient's Bill of Rights

An important document, which can provide you with guidelines on hospital procedures and ways in which you can deal with them, is the Pregnant Patient's Bill of Rights and Responsibilities prepared by the International Childbirth Education Association. It is reprinted in the appendix.

The bill outlines a pregnant patient's right to be clearly informed about the nature of any suggested drug treatment or any procedure or therapy—its safety, its effects, its dangers to her or the baby, alternatives to the treatment, the name and qualifications of the person administering the treatment, and the full right, without pressure from any medical personnel, to refuse any treatment. While it is not law, this concept of informed consent—thoroughly informing patients about proposed medicines and treatments—is also strongly supported and promoted by The American College of Obstetricians and Gynecologists in its *Standards for Obstetric Gynecologic Services.*

Many times during labor and delivery, a woman is given medication she does not require. This happens to women who have not taken childbirth preparation classes, and also to those who have participated in classes and are familiar with ways of helping themselves during the rougher moments.

Our experience can serve as an example. When Kathy was in labor with Kristen, she reluctantly agreed to receive a last-minute anesthetic, which proved to be unnecessary and ultimately very painful. Kathy had been in labor for over six hours and her cervix was almost completely dilated. She was having a particularly difficult time because the baby's head was in a posterior position (facing up rather than down), and this made it more difficult for the baby to pass through the birth canal. For Kathy, it meant she had to push very hard to get the baby safely through the canal. When the baby's head finally crowned her birth was imminent. Kathy had gotten this far without any medication to reduce labor pains, and it looked as if she would persevere through to the birth without medication. However, the attending nurse asked Kathy if she wanted a spinal anesthetic—a saddle-block—to get her through the birth. With all the confusion of the last phase of labor before the birth, Kathy and I weren't aware just how close she actually was to giving birth. We didn't realize that the baby was almost ready to burst through the birth canal. Her head was quite visible. The most difficult part of labor was almost over. If a mother makes it this far without an anesthetic, she usually is able to continue on in the same manner. Having had a rough go of it the last few hours and being totally exhausted, Kathy looked up at me and said "Sean, what do you think? Shall I take it?" Before I could say anything the nurse snapped at Kathy, "What are you asking him for? He's not having the baby." I sheepishly remained silent, bewildered and angry, afraid to open my mouth. I felt like I was being treated like an outsider, one who shouldn't be there in the first place. Finally, I said softly, "Whatever you decide is okay." Not receiving any encouragement to consider refusing the nurse's offer, Kathy agreed to have the saddle-block. Fifteen minutes later, our daughter Kristen was born. Kristen was healthy and looked beautiful—Kathy and I were overjoyed. Shortly after Kristen's birth, however, we realized how deeply we regretted not fully discussing the offer of the anesthetic. If we had had a moment to confer, Kathy told me, she would not have taken it. It was totally unnecessary and, unfortunately, very painful—it caused Kathy severe headaches for weeks afterward.

Being familiar with the Pregnant Patient's Bill of Rights may help you and your wife if, in a similar situation, you are confronted with the decision as to whether or not to take a suggested medication. But remember—the flip side of the Bill of Rights is The Pregnant Patient's Responsibilities. You must be informed and knowledgeable if you plan to make your own decisions.

## Don't Forget a Pediatrician

Sometimes in the excitement of preparing for childbirth, expectant parents put off the decision to choose a pediatrician. Many feel this can be done soon enough after the birth. As with your choice of an obstetrician, your choice of a pediatrician is important because you want one who is competent, experienced, and whose philosophy or approach you are comfortable with. Your early decision regarding a pediatrician is doubly important because you will want his or her services in examining your newborn immediately and carefully observing his progress during those first hours and days. Should any complication arise, you can rely on someone you've carefully chosen and not worry about the abilities and experience of someone who has been routinely assigned. If the pediatrician you choose is not affiliated with the hospital where your baby will be born, ask him to recommend a colleague of his who has privileges at your hospital. To have someone recommended by your pediatrician to cover for him during the days your wife and baby will be at the hospital is commonly done, especially in areas of the country where there are lots of hospitals.

In choosing a pediatrician, find out if he is board-certified by your state's medical board and/or if he is a fellow of the American Academy of Pediatrics. This indicates he's received specialized training and keeps abreast of the latest developments in his field through formal educational programs. Also consult other parents for their recommendations. Other parents can give you an account of their experiences and impressions of the pediatrician they bring their children to.

Arrange to meet him and find out how he approaches his practice and if you feel comfortable with him. Dr. Joel Sussman, a pediatrician in Columbia, South Carolina, meets regularly with groups of expectant parents as well as with other parents who have been recommended to him. In a preliminary two-hour evening meeting with a small group, he explains to the expectant parents his philosophy of caring for his patients, the general practices he follows, the practices he recommends, for example, the use of car seats for children, the arrangements he and his associate have to ensure that their patients are covered 24 hours a day, and his billing procedures. During the two-hour session, he answers questions about all aspects of his practice. Often he'll spend lots of time talking about newborns and the services he provides for them during their brief stay at the hospital.

More and more pediatricians are in joint practice with pediatric nurse practitioners or pediatric nurse clinicians—nurses with specialized training in pediatrics. If you find a pediatrician in such a joint practice, you'll find that the nurse practitioner is more accessible to patients for routine matters. This is by design, so he or she can devote time to educating parents about good health care of children, while the pediatrician concentrates on the more highly specialized tasks of medical care. The nurse practitioner in practice with our pediatrician at the time of our daughter Kristen's birth came to the hospital every day, spent lots of time answering our questions about Kristen, and was a constant source of encouragement and solid advice during those exciting and baffling first weeks and months.

## Childbirth Education Classes

A major factor in the successful delivery or birth of your child is for your wife to be confident, relaxed, and prepared both physically and psychologically. Your wife's obstetrician will more than likely recommend that both she and you attend a childbirth education course at some time in the middle of the third trimester. Studies have shown that if a woman is adequately prepared for childbirth, chances are greater that she will have an easier time of it and fewer complications than women who are not prepared. For an expectant mother, childbirth preparation should begin early and include good nutrition, exercise, plenty of rest, a positive attitude toward pregnancy, support from her husband and family, knowledge of the physiological and psychological changes taking place within her, and an understanding of what will occur during labor and delivery. Childbirth preparation classes generally are offered to women and their husbands during the last two months before the birth and focus on labor and delivery, the physiological aspects of the birth, various breathing and relaxing techniques identified with the childbirth approach you are learning, and how husbands can play an instrumental role in offering physical and moral support to their wives.

A growing number of childbirth preparation courses across the country are offered, in part, earlier during pregnancy, and focus not only on childbirth but also on the challenges of the early weeks as a parent. These courses cover baby care skills and some continue up to six or eight weeks after the birth and deal with the major adjustments of becoming parents.

Childbirth preparation courses can be enormously helpful to you. If they are well organized and taught well, they will present to you a clear picture of what to expect during your wife's labor and delivery and practical ways you can assist her. Courses are offered in virtually every community across the country by such sponsors as hospitals, childbirth education organizations, individual obstetricians, and other groups.

Find out what choices are available to you in your region. Are courses offered by the hospital; your obstetrician; organizations such as the American Society for Psychoprophylaxis in Obstetrics (ASPO), which promotes the Lamaze method of prepared childbirth; the American Academy of Husband-Coached Childbirth or the Bradley Method; or some other organization? Read as much as you can about the courses and methods the various sponsors use in approaching childbirth. (See the last part of this chapter for information about some of the more popular methods of approaching childbirth and whom you can contact to find out what courses are offered in your region.) Again, your wife's views should have greater weight than yours in deciding what method or approach to childbirth she will follow. But you should have a significant input as well. So, the two of you should discuss the choices available to you and explore these possibilities with each other's concerns in mind.

Contact several childbirth preparation instructors by phone or in person and inquire about their courses. If, once initial phone inquiries are made, two or three good choices are available, arrange for both of you to meet the instructors. It may seem like a nuisance at first to spend all this time in deciding on what instructor to choose, but it will prove very helpful later. During the last month or so of pregnancy, there are added worries and concerns, and being with other expectant parents in a class taught by a knowledgeable and supportive instructor can be an invaluable boost to your wife and you as the tension builds with the approach of the day of delivery. Although most instructors are well informed about childbirth and many are women who have been through the experience themselves, they may not be good teachers or may not be able to adapt their material to the wide variety of expectant parents who take their courses. In addition to having a competent teacher, you will find it most helpful if your instructor is someone with whom you feel comfortable, someone whose personality and outlook is compatible with your wife's and yours.

To help you determine your choice of an instructor, consider some of these questions.

- *What kind of training has she received to teach childbirth preparation classes? Has she received training from and is she certified by the American Society for Psychoprophylaxis in Obstetrics, the International Childbirth Education Association, the American Academy of Husband-Coached Childbirth, or some other legitimate organization or institution? Does she participate in any continuing education programs within her field that keep her abreast of current research and practices regarding childbirth?*
- *Has she had children herself and what kind of birth experience has she had?*
- *Ask her to give you a brief rundown of what material is covered in the course. A solid childbirth preparation course that also includes classes after the birth dealing with the adjustments new parents face could prove invaluable to both of you. As good and as popular as most childbirth preparation*

courses are across the country, they quite naturally focus on the birth itself and often neglect what comes afterward. For many expectant parents, there is a big letdown after the birth because they've not been adequately prepared for the sometimes difficult challenges of the first few weeks home with the baby.

- *What is her attitude toward an expectant father's role during his wife's labor and delivery?*
- *What does the course cost?*
- *Is a tour of an obstetrical facility of a hospital part of the course?*
- *Will she accompany you to the hospital and attend the birth if you so desire? What would the fee be for this additional service?*
- *Are any films shown during the course? Some films are excellent and a great aid in preparing for labor and delivery.*
- *When is the course offered and how long does it last? Most courses are offered one evening a week for six weeks, and it is recommended you begin taking them about seven or eight weeks before your wife's due date. If a course is available to you earlier, it is recommended. There is an increasing number of courses offered that begin in early pregnancy, last a few weeks, and then are continued during the last five or six weeks of pregnancy.*
- *How large are the classes? Are they of manageable size? The courses impart much critical information, but one of their most important functions is to give expectant parents the opportunity to share their experiences, to benefit from knowing they aren't alone. If there are more than 18 persons in the class, it is too difficult for everyone to participate fully.*
- *Is time allocated for discussion and free exchanges among the persons in the class? If your wife and you are new residents of an area or if you don't have much contact with other expectant parents, having the extra time in class will enable you to meet new friends. This may be even more important for you, especially if you have serious reservations about your participation during labor and delivery. You'll meet other men whose attitudes and views are similar to yours, as well as men who have few if any reservations about being with their wives during the birth. The combination of taking the course and meeting these other men will help you sort out your feelings and very likely resolve any doubts or reservations you may have.*

# Approaches to Childbirth

## The Lamaze Method

One of the most widely known approaches to childbirth is the Lamaze method of prepared childbirth, which was first popularized by Paris obstetrician Fernand Lamaze in the early 1950s. It is called psychoprophylactic childbirth preparation because it involves psychological and physiological preparation that fosters childbirth with little or no medical intervention and few if any drugs during labor and delivery. It is an active technique involving special breathing, exercises, muscle relaxing, and massage techniques that serve to distract the mother and aid her in dealing with any fear or pain caused through the contractions and rigors of labor. The husband has a significant role in orchestrating the use of the techniques by timing contractions and encouraging his wife to do the breathing and relaxing exercises properly.

Dr. Lamaze based his technique of prepared childbirth on the Pavlovian principles of conditioned responses developed at the Pavlov Institute in Russia and used for preparing expectant mothers for childbirth. Dr. Lamaze visited Russia and studied this method in 1951, and later introduced the technique to France and other West European countries. In 1959 Majorie Karmel introduced the Lamaze method to the United States in her bestseller *Thank You, Dr. Lamaze.* In 1960 she and Elisabeth Bing founded the American Society for Psychoprophylaxis in Obstetrics (ASPO), an organization dedicated to promoting prepared childbirth through the use of the Lamaze method. According to Elisabeth Bing, ASPO was at first a medical society but soon became a broader-based organization of childbirth education professionals, physicians, and parents. With over 8000 members, more than 60 percent of whom are certified childbirth educators, ASPO trains close to one million expectant mothers and fathers each year. The childbirth preparation course (Lamaze method) offered through ASPO views an expectant mother and father as a team and sees the father's role as active and supportive. Accordingly, a father is urged to know as much about childbirth and about how to use the Lamaze technique as his wife does so he will be able to offer his continuous support throughout labor and delivery.

*For information about the Lamaze approach to childbirth and courses offered by ASPO in your area, contact the national headquarters of ASPO:*

**American Society for Psychoprophylaxis in Obstetrics**
1411 K Street, N. W.
Washington, DC 20005
(202) 783-7050

See the appendix for a complete listing of ASPO chapters in the United States. For a referral to a group, certified childbirth educator, or supportive physician in an area not listed in the appendix, contact the ASPO National Information and Referral Service at the address given above.

## Bradley Method

Developed by Dr. Robert Bradley, a Denver obstetrician and author of *Husband-Coached Childbirth,* the Bradley method involves training expectant mothers to deal with the tension and fears of labor and delivery by being able to reduce these through relaxed breathing and the constant positive support of their husbands. The method teaches the expectant mother to relax and to be fully aware of her body and all that she is experiencing throughout labor and delivery. Rather than trying to distract her in order to get through each contraction, a woman learns to relax in such a way as not only to be more aware of the contraction but in the process to reduce any pain associated with it. The underlying philosophy of this approach is that the chief obstacle to pregnancy is fear, which can severely interfere with what should be a beautiful, natural experience. According to Dr. Bradley, animals intuitively give birth in a natural, relaxed way, but women must be taught to relax.

One of the goals of the Bradley method is for an expectant mother to give birth without the use of any drugs. Drugs, says Dr. Bradley, no matter in what quantity or how they are received, can have a potentially harmful effect on an unborn baby.

Dr. Bradley's method is strongly influenced by the work of a pioneer in childbirth education, the late Dr. Grantly Dick-Read, a British obstetrician who wrote *Childbirth Without Fear: The Principles and Practice of Natural Childbirth,* a classic work detailing an approach to childbirth that focuses on methods of relaxation that help overcome tension and pain brought about by fear. Adopting many of the principles of Grantly Dick-Read, the Bradley method puts a great deal more emphasis on the role of the father than does the Dick-Read approach, calling the method "husband-coached childbirth."

The Bradley method is more widespread in the western region of the United States, especially in California, but it is gaining in popularity in other parts of the country, particularly in the Northeast and the South.

*For more information about this husband-oriented approach to prepared childbirth, and about courses offered by the American Academy of Husband-Coached Childbirth in your region, write to:*

**American Academy of Husband-Coached Childbirth**
P. O. Box 5224
Sherman Oaks, CA 91413

## The Leboyer Approach

Dr. Frederick Leboyer, a French obstetrician and author of *Birth Without Violence,* has developed an approach to childbirth, which, he believes, creates a joyful, peaceful atmosphere for a baby's first moments outside the womb. Like Dr. Lamaze, Dr. Leboyer is interested in promoting a healthy, relaxed birth experience. Lamaze's approach, however, has focused on the expectant mother and father, and Leboyer's has focused on the newborn child. Using Leboyer's approach, a baby is born in a room with dimmed lights and soft music, and then, before the umbilical cord is cut, is placed immediately face down on his mother's bare abdomen. After a few minutes, the baby is immersed, usually by his father, in a specially prepared warm-water bath. Many of Leboyer's techniques are being used in whole or in part by parents across the country. They are compatible with most methods of childbirth. If you are interested in using some or all of these techniques, make this request of your obstetrician and try to work out the details with him or her.

*For more information about the Leboyer method, write:*

**National Association for the Advancement of Leboyer's Birth without Violence**
P. O. Box 248455
Miami, FL 33124

*Or write to ASPO (page 76) or ICEA headquarters (below).*

## Sources of Information

### International Childbirth Education Association (ICEA)

Founded in 1960 at the first National Convention for Childbirth Education in Milwaukee, the International Childbirth Education Association is a consumer-oriented organization of hundreds of childbirth preparation educators, parents, professional groups, and thousands of individuals around the world. ICEA focuses on every aspect of childbirth—the educational, physical, and emotional preparation of expectant parents for childbirth; the training of childbirth educators, the promotion among hospitals and medical personnnel of prepared childbirth with minimal obstetric intervention; and the study and promotion of family-centered maternity and child care. Tied in naturally with its focus on childbirth is ICEA's dedication to all aspects of preparing parents for their introduction to parenthood.

ICEA's motto is "Freedom of choice based on knowledge of alternatives." Significantly, it promotes no particular method or approach to childbirth, has members representing a broad range of viewpoints and concerns, and has established a lively dialogue between providers and consumers of health care on the issues related to childbearing. With over 12,000 members, most of whom are from the United States, ICEA is the largest consumer-oriented childbirth education organization and an important source of information for your wife and you about every aspect of childbirth.

*For more information about ICEA and childbirth preparation programs in your city or town, write to ICEA's headquarters:*

**International Childbirth Education Association**
P. O. Box 20048
Minneapolis, MN 55420

*See the appendix for a detailed listing for the regional organizations affiliated with ICEA in the United States and Canada.*

## For Cesarean Couples

Many fathers look forward to being present at the birth of their children and in spending time with their wives and newborns immediately after the birth. Today, having a cesarean birth does not have to mean the end to these plans.

Since 1972, C/SEC has been influential in promoting fathers' participation in cesarean deliveries. This organization also offers emotional and educational support for cesarian parents by phone, correspondence, literature, audio-visual material, and hospital workshops. *For information, contact:*

**Cesareans/Support, Education and Concern (C/SEC)**
66 Christopher Road
Waltham, MA 02154
(617) 547-7188

If you are interested in learning about avoiding primary cesareans, in having a vaginal birth after a cesarean, and in receiving emotional support for anticipated or past cesareans, this group can help:

**Cesarean Educational Alliance (CEA)**
Journey's End Road
Francestown, NH 03043
(603) 547-2095

## La Leche League

La Leche League was founded to instruct and encourage mothers who want to breast-feed their babies. Fathers whose wives are breast-feeding can receive information and support from this organization. *Write to:*

**La Leche League, International (LLLI)**
9616 Minneapolis Avenue
Franklin Park, IL 60131

# Alternative Birth Centers/Alternative Birth Choices

In the past 20 years the consumer-oriented childbirth education movement has laid the groundwork for the increasing number of choices women now have regarding how and where they will give birth to their children. Most women still have their babies in hospitals, but during the past few years there has been a dramatic increase in the number of women who are choosing to have their babies at alternative birth centers or at home.

Alternative birth centers have been established within hospitals or as separate entities in many regions of the country to provide a safe, homelike atmosphere for women who represent low-risk pregnancies. Many of these centers are staffed by certified nurse midwives who are specially trained in obstetrics. Their services are generally significantly cheaper than those of a traditional hospital delivery-room setting. And at many in-hospital or out-of-hospital centers, women may leave between 12 and 24 hours after delivery, further reducing the costs of childbirth. Should complications arise while delivering at an alternative birth center within a hospital, a woman has access to the services of medical doctors, who routinely offer backup support to the nurse midwives in emergencies, and to any hospital equipment that may be needed. Equally good backup support is offered by many of the alternative birth centers that exist separately from hospitals.

The home birth movement, too, is currently gathering strength in the United States. According to its proponents, with the proper prenatal screenings by an experienced doctor or midwife and with emergency backup support (transportation and equipment), women can safely give birth at home.

*For more information about alternatives in childbirth, write to:*

**American Academy of Husband-Coached Childbirth (AAHCC)**
Box 5224
Sherman Oaks, CA 91413

**American College of Home Obstetrics (ACHO)**
664 North Michigan Avenue,
Suite 600
Chicago, IL 60611

**American College of Nurse-Midwifery (ACNM)**
1000 Vermont Avenue, N.W.
Washington, DC 20005

**American Society for Psychoprophylaxis in Obstetrics (ASPO)**
1411 K Street, N.W.
Washington, DC 20005

**Association for Childbirth at Home (ACHI)**
P. O. Box 1219
Cerritos, CA 90701

**Childbirth without Pain Education Association (CWPEA)**
20134 Snowden
Detroit, MI 48235

**Childbirth without Pain Education League (CWPEL)**
3940 11th Street
Riverside, CA 92501

**Home Oriented Maternity Experience (HOME)**
511 New York Avenue
Takoma Park
Washington, DC 20012

**International Childbirth Education Association (ICEA)**
P. O. Box 20048
Minneapolis, MN 55420

**The Farm**
156 Drakes Lane
Summertown, TN 38483

**Maternity Center Association**
48 East 92nd Street
New York, NY 10028

**National Association of Parents and Professionals for Safe Alternatives in Childbirth (NAPSAC)**
P. O. Box 267
Marble Hill, MO 63764

**National Midwives Association**
P. O. Box 163
Princeton, NJ 08540

**Society for the Protection of the Unborn through Nutrition (SPUN)**
17 North Wabash, Suite 603
Chicago, IL 60602

# The Expectant Father on Delivery Day

# Be Prepared!

Keiichi and Kathy Morrell of Anaheim, California, had already attended prepared childbirth classes and were looking forward to the birth of their third child who was expected on December 13, 1979. They were experienced, knew what signs would indicate that Kathy was in labor and ready to go to the hospital. However, on two occasions in early November Kathy felt some discomfort. To be on the safe side, she reported to the hospital where she was examined, told she wasn't ready yet, and sent home.

On Veteran's Day, November 11, Kathy again felt some discomfort but thought it was just another false alarm and didn't go back to the hospital. This time the discomfort persisted: She knew she was suddenly experiencing actual labor. It was late morning and there was no time to contact her husband who had already gone to work. Fortunately, her two sons were home from school, so she had them call for a paramedic team and an ambulance. But her labor was progressing so quickly, there was no time to wait for help. As eight-year-old Chuck received instructions over the phone from Anaheim Police Sergeant Franklin Van De Weerd, he relayed them to 13-year-old brother Jimmy who was assisting his mother. After less than a half-hour, Chuck shouted to Sergeant Van De Weerd, "The baby's out!" The sergeant had a few more instructions relayed, and Jimmy calmly cleared the baby's throat and nose. Chuck reported to the sergeant that the baby was crying. "Is it a boy or a girl?" asked the sergeant. "I don't know," replied Chuck. It was a boy, Keiichi Morrell, Jr., and shortly after his rapid birth he and his mother were taken to the hospital, both in good condition.

The story of Keiichi Morrell, Jr.'s birth received national coverage. It was a story filled with tension and drama and one with a very happy ending. It is similar to many of the dramatic birth stories reported frequently—stories of births in taxi cabs, on trains, in subway cars, and in many other unusual locations. The chances that your wife will have such a quick labor and delivery are rare, especially if it's her first child. Labor and delivery for a first child average from twelve to fourteen hours. The average time for a second child is seven or eight hours. But since there are so many stories around about first-time mothers who have had dramatically short labor periods, it pays to be well prepared. Stories also abound about mothers who have misinterpreted the telltale signs indicating the onset of labor.

To avoid any mix-ups, during the last four or five weeks before the due date, arrange to be easy to reach so you may be by your wife's side as soon as possible when she needs you. If your work involves travel, try to arrange to stay close to the home office; and if you cannot be reached by phone at your place of work, arrange for some contact person to be available to get hold of you when needed. You don't want to miss the birth of your child should your wife's labor be shorter than anticipated, but more important, you want to be with your wife because she needs your active support.

# Labor

In addition to being available to your wife, it can be of enormous help if you know as much as you can about the phenomenon of labor—what happens biologically, the signs indicating when labor begins, and how you can best assist your wife throughout. During the labor period, you will witness the most outwardly dramatic and intense moments of pregnancy.

You should easily be able to gain a basic understanding of the biological mechanics of what happens during labor. Why labor begins when it does, however, is another matter and has never been answered completely. When you are learning what takes place in labor and how you can help your wife, keep in mind that the biological knowledge enshrouds the mystery of pregnancy and birth. However important, this knowledge is hollow if not accompanied by the sense of mystery. This mystery exists in all life and you are sharing it in a special way through the birth of your child.

For a pregnant woman, labor is defined as the intense period at the end of pregnancy when her uterus changes shape or contracts to make way for her baby's exit. For the baby, it is the intense period during which he makes the radical transition to a life dependent on the full functioning of his own life-support system. Labor begins when the oxygen in the placenta starts to decrease sharply, triggering the end of the supply of progesterone, the hormone that has helped maintain the pregnancy. This, in turn, causes the muscles in the uterus to begin contracting. In a series of complex processes, the baby, who's now begun to lose his uterine life-support system, starts making the transition to living independently of his mother. His respiratory, digestive, and nervous systems begin functioning more vigorously and independently. All this occurs while the baby is being forced slowly by the contracting uterus toward the opening of the birth canal. As he's being pressured on all sides by the uterine walls, the contractions are also gradually causing the cervix and cervical canal to open. The opening increases in size from its usual 1/2 centimeter (3/8 inch) to approximately 10 centimeters (4 inches), just wide enough for the baby's head to emerge safely.

In a gentler form, an expectant mother has been experiencing contractions of her uterus many weeks before labor begins. These are called Braxton-Hicks contractions, and it is thought that their purpose is to strengthen the uterine muscles in preparation for labor.

The contractions of the uterus during labor are generally more intense than the Braxton-Hicks contractions are, and they are one of the most significant indications that the final stage of pregnancy is at hand. At first, the contractions, which occur in rhythmic cycles, may last 15 to 25 seconds and come 10 to 15 minutes apart. Sometimes at this stage they go unnoticed because they are so mild. They soon begin to occur closer and closer together, about 3 to 5 minutes apart, and become longer and stronger. They are characterized by a tightening of the uterine muscles, which increases in intensity and then gradually fades away. Some women have compared them to the rising, breaking, and falling of waves on the shore of the ocean. They can also be accompanied by a variety of symptoms: The contractions can be felt first in the region of the lower back, they can be felt as menstrual-like cramps, and they can be accompanied by a discharge of mucuous with a stain of blood (sometimes called a "show") and a discharge of fluid. This fluid, in which the baby has been developing, had been held in place by the fetal amniotic membrance (bag of waters), which usually ruptures during the early stages of labor. Another possible early sign of labor is the urge to push.

When it is determined that your wife is indeed having contractions, begin timing them. When you do so, consider their frequency (how many minutes from the beginning of one contraction to the beginning of the next), their duration (how long they last from the beginning of a contraction to its cessation), and their intensity (the strength of the contraction). When the contractions are quite regular and start occuring closer together, lasting longer and getting stronger, have your wife call the obstetrician, or you call if she would like you to. The obstetrician most likely will have suggested when to call him, but a good rule of thumb is for your wife or you to call whenever there are any serious doubts or questions about what's happening to your wife. And don't be worried that you may disturb him unnecessarily. If you have questions and doubts about what's happening, it is necessary to call. He or she is expecting to hear from you, and it is better to be safe than late.

## Assisting During Labor

Beginning in the 1920s and 1930s, when the majority of American women began having their babies in hospitals and not at home, we were not permitted to be with our wives during labor and delivery. We were segregated and treated as helpless figures who could only pace hallways and pester the hospital staff for news of any progress. We were considered incapable of helping our wives in any way. Now, thanks to the phenomenal growth and influence of the childbirth education movement during the last two decades, our role as fathers during childbirth has changed dramatically: We can be where we should be when our children are born—with our wives—and we can assist in very significant ways.

One of the most important ways you can help your wife during her pregnancy, but particularly during labor, is to offer her strong emotional support. She needs it because of the fears associated with childbirth, fears that may even make a stronger impact on her if this is her first child and she doesn't have any close friends who have already had children. Her questions may be many. Can I make it through labor? Will I get to the hospital in time? Will I be able to reach my husband in time? Suppose I can't and I have to be alone? Will the baby be all right? Can I make it through labor without taking an anesthetic? These are only some of the questions mothers ask that reflect their fears and concerns, and they are valid questions. Childbirth is serious, sacred, beautiful, but not without its risks. It is also a natural human process

# SIGNS OF LABOR

*If you know the symptoms associated with the on-set of labor, you will be in a better position to advise and support your wife. Your wife's doctor will suggest when you should call him, but it's always best to call him whenever anything happens that you can't understand or whenever you have serious questions.*

## True Labor

1. Contractions will occur regularly with increasing frequency, duration, and intensity. Discomfort resulting from the contractions may first be felt in the lower back or in the lower abdomen, above the pubic bone.
2. "Show"—a discharge of blood-stained mucous may occur.
3. Discharge of fluid from the fetal amniotic membrane or bag of waters.
4. The cervix opening increases beyond its normal 1-centimeter diameter (the doctor will have to determine this).

## False Labor

1. Contractions may be regular or irregular but they do not change in frequency, duration, or intensity. Discomfort is usually experienced in the abdominal area.
2. Usually no show or discharge of any fluid.
3. The cervix is undilated.

*Always keep in close touch with the obstetrician*

and women are innately endowed with the strength and courage needed to bear children in that process. Unfortunately, neither women nor the childbirth process itself has been respected enough. When hospital births became popular in the 1920s and 1930s, expectant mothers, through the very nature of the artificial setting of the hospital, were looked upon as patients in need of treatment, not as healthy women who wanted to have the childbirth process completed in a setting that provided the backup support of technology should it ever be needed. Childbirth was looked at as a medical rather than a natural phenomenon.

Hospitals are safe settings for childbirth, and they have made great strides in the past ten years to make their maternity units more humane, yet fears of pregnancy and childbirth still are widespread. One way to help your wife combat these fears, no matter what their source, is to approach pregnancy positively. A friend of mine told me how she and her husband dealt with the atmosphere that surrounded them early during her pregnancy. When she told her friends the good news that she was pregnant, she received the expected congratulatory greetings but she also received many condolences. Her friends told her how difficult pregnancy would be, warned her about this and that, and told her to keep her chin up—they knew what she was going through. My friend became angry and frightened. Eventually she confided in a neighbor of hers who had two boys. The neighbor was quite positive about having gone through pregnancy and told her how much she enjoyed it, how exciting it was, and how any discomforts were minor compared to the joys. My friend, with encouragement from her husband, began feeling very optimistic about her pregnancy and finally had her child without the problems her friends had predicted. Her secret, she told me, was having a positive attitude. This positive attitude didn't eliminate all her fears but it did help her realize that pregnancy wasn't the unmitigated horror some of her friends warned her about. Both she and her husband became well informed about all aspects of pregnancy and basically saw it more realistically.

If you have this positive outlook going into the final six or seven weeks of your wife's pregnancy, it's terrific. But sometimes you may encounter another type of pervasive fear that can be spread by medical personnel and medically oriented childbirth educators. One teacher of a prepared childbirth class I visited told her class it was unrealistic for women to have as a goal to go through labor without assistance from drugs or some other form of medical intervention. A nurse by training, who had had several children herself, she contradicted the basic principles of the approach to natural childbirth she was supposed to be espousing. She encouraged long discussions in her class of every conceivable mishap that could occur during labor and delivery in order to "prepare" them. She appeared cheery and upbeat but her underlying message was one of fear. One of her students, an expectant mother who had had a very positive experience with the birth of her first child, said she would often leave class sessions frightened and angry. She and her husband combatted this fear by their deep belief, based on their

# LABOR KIT

*Several weeks before your wife's due date, assemble a labor kit of things you and your wife may wish to use at the hospital. The objects you choose will be determined by your own needs and the recommendations made by your childbirth educator. Below is a suggested checklist of items.*

1. A watch with a second hand—to time contractions and to monitor the breathing techniques your wife will use.

2. Lip balm—to apply to your wife's lips when they become dry.

3. Sour lollipop—helps moisten your wife's mouth, which can get very dry and uncomfortable.

4. Talcum powder or cornstarch—to use when you are rubbing your wife's legs, back, and arms.

5. Tennis balls in sock or rolling pin—helpful to use on your wife's back to relieve tension and pain.

6. Pen and paper—to jot down the time when timing the contractions.

7. Insurance policy numbers. Try to arrange beforehand for your wife to register at the hospital. This is usually done through the obstetrician's office. More important, though, is to arrange with the hospital that you will not be separated from your wife when you arrive there. Every childbirth educator can tell you stories of fathers who missed the births of their children because they were tied up in the admissions office signing papers. Also, your wife needs your support as she enters the unknown and often threatening environment of a hospital.

8. Thermos and snacks—you need to keep up your strength and you might not want to leave your wife's side.

9. Coins—for phone calls and snacks.

10. Phone numbers—to make calls after the birth.
    If you forget everything on your prepared list, don't worry. The most important thing for your wife at this time is to have you by her side. Your active presence is worth more than all the suggested items, however helpful they may be. Fortunately, most hospitals are well equipped for the hundreds of thousands of mothers and fathers who have gone through childbirth education programs, so you will most likely be able to get a few of the items you're most in need of.

previous experience, that if they expected a safe, trouble-free labor and birth, their chances of this happening would be greater. Their expectations were fulfilled. Being well informed about pregnancy and childbirth, however, they knew that unexpected complications can occur no matter what one's expectations.

If you are aware of the natural and unnatural fears surrounding pregnancy and childbirth, you can respond more appropriately to your wife's needs as she enters labor. Specific examples of what you may possibly do could include: assuring her everything's going to be all right; telling her you love her and believe in her; holding and caressing her; acting as liaison between her and her doctor and the hospital staff; and being responsible for all the small details involved in getting to the hospital with all the aids you'll need to help your wife during labor. Put differently, do everything and anything you feel you need to do to help your wife: You will help reduce any unnecessary anxiety; you and your wife will come closer together; the baby will have an easier go of it; and the two of you will add immeasurably to the incredible joy of being together at the birth of your child.

## Labor: A Personal Account

In July 1979, my wife Kathy gave birth to our second child, Geoffrey. We were again reminded that textbook descriptions of what is supposed to happen during labor and delivery do not necessarily correspond to the reality. The books we read and the classes we attended were generally helpful, but we felt there was a gap between what we had learned and what we actually experienced during labor and birth. The writers and teachers failed to emphasize the need to be flexible and rely strongly on your intelligence and basic instincts. So let me say it now, strongly and clearly: Read as much as you can about pregnancy, labor, and childbirth, go to childbirth education classes, but, most important of all, trust your instincts, be prepared for the unexpected, and have confidence and trust in your wife who has been blessed with an innate strength you are soon to witness.

A Vermont nurse practitioner with whom I worked several years ago told me there's no such thing as a baby being born late. "Babies," she said, "are born when they're good and ready to be born. Not before. Not later. It's nature's law." Due dates set by obstetricians are rough approximations and can be off by as much as several weeks on either side. But their necessary existence can cause you and your wife needless anxiety, particularly when your wife is "overdue." When our first child, Kristen, was "late" in being born—three weeks past the due date—Kathy and I were terribly anxious. The expectations and suspense kept building and building, added to greatly by inquiries from friends, "What happened?" "When's the baby coming?" "You didn't have that baby yet!" When our second child, Geoffrey, was late in being born, Kathy and I took it in stride, figuring he'd be born when he

# THREE STAGES OF LABOR:

## WHAT FATHERS CAN DO TO HELP

## FIRST STAGE

*During the first stage, the uterus contracts, causing the cervix to efface (gradually becoming thinner and shorter) and dilate (opening to approximately 10 centimeters or 4 inches). The first stage lasts on the average of 12 to 14 hours for first births and an average of 7 hours for subsequent ones. There are three phases to the first stage: early labor, active labor, and transition.*

### Early Labor

Be there with your wife. Make sure she's comfortable, that she rests between contractions to save her strength for later, and that she is as free from worry as possible. When the contractions get closer and closer together—10 minutes or less—call your doctor. In fact, call your doctor whenever you have any questions or doubts about what is happening to your wife.

Time the contractions: their frequency (how many minutes apart they are), their duration (how long they last), and their intensity (how strong they are).

Go to the hospital or maternity center when the doctor recommends it, or, if you can't reach him right away, when the contractions are 5 minutes or less apart.

Gather together the items you'll need at the hospital and make all other last-minute arrangements. Use your judgment, though—start out earlier if the weather is bad, if you live far from the hospital, or if you have to bring older children to the place they'll be staying while you are at the hospital.

## Active Labor

During active labor, the contractions occur 3 to 5 minutes apart, last up to 60 seconds, are intense, and the cervix dilates to 4–7 centimeters.

Labor speeds up a bit, but you may still have hours to wait, and in many hospitals, you and your wife will be alone much of the time, with periodic visits from hospital staff members. You can help in an important way by being the liaison between your wife and the staff members, making requests for assistance for her, seeking advice for how to help out more effectively if a problem arises.

If your wife begins to get tense and rigid, help her relax by holding her and by rubbing her back, shoulders, arms, legs, or lower abdomen (effleurage).

When her mouth gets dry, give her some ice chips or a sip of fresh water or a taste of a sour-flavored lollipop.

Help her change position when needed.

Continue to encourage her.

Continue timing the contractions.

Monitor the breathing or relaxation techniques you both have learned for the various phases of labor.

## Transition

During transition, usually one of the most intense periods of labor, the cervix becomes completely dilated to 10 centimeters (4 inches). Transition is brief: There are generally 10 to 20 contractions that occur about every 2 minutes, are extremely intense, and last 60 to 90 seconds each.

Lots of encouragement needed.

Firm guidance regarding the breathing and relaxation techniques. If you are following the Lamaze method, the pant-blow breathing technique is quite effective at this time.

Take your cue as to how to help during this intense period from the hospital staff assisting your wife.

Tell your wife she's almost through: Take one contraction at a time.

Don't be alarmed at your wife if she becomes quite irritable, yells at you, or does not want you to touch her during this phase. Remember, the next stage of labor, which is about to happen very soon, is the birth of the baby.

# SECOND STAGE

*The second stage of labor is the birth of the baby. The cervix is fully dilated and the baby begins its passage through the birth canal.*

Continue encouraging your wife.

Tell her of the progress she is making as she pushes when instructed by the obstetrician or midwife. She will most likely be in an awkward position to see the baby's head crown and the baby's progress as it slowly makes its way out from the birth canal.

The baby is born. He or she will be placed in your wife's arms and covered. Ad lib. Do whatever comes naturally, but don't forget your wife in the excitement of rejoicing over the baby—she still needs your affection and your attention, especially during the anticlimatic period immediately after the birth.

# THIRD STAGE

The uterus continues to contract, a process that helps to expel the placenta within five minutes after the birth and later brings about the reduction of the uterus to its normal shape. The uterine contractions also help stop the bleeding caused when the placenta is torn from the uterine wall. The doctor, who has already quickly examined the baby, will carefully examine the placenta. Continue enjoying these precious moments with your wife and newborn child.

was ready. We played down the original due date our obstetrician gave us so as not to encourage needless anxiety.

When the real due date occurs, it still catches you by surprise, regardless of how prepared you are. When Kathy was pregnant with our son, Geoffrey, we felt we were quite well prepared: We had already had one child; Kathy was "overdue" so we knew she would be going into labor sometime within a few weeks; and we thought we knew what signs to look for that would tell us labor had begun. We were again taken by surprise.

Around 3:30 A.M. on July 27, Kathy, three days overdue, awoke feeling sick. During the last few months, Kathy had been feeling great. She had been swimming about 1/4 mile each day throughout the pregnancy and she was in terrific shape. Kathy rushed to the bathroom, hoping that if she urinated, her bladder would deflate and relieve some of the pressure in her lower abdomen. She felt a little better and returned to bed. Around 4 A.M. she tapped me on the shoulder, saying, "Sean, I think something's happening but I don't know what."

"What are you feeling?" I asked.

"I don't know exactly. It doesn't feel like contractions. I feel some pain way down here where the baby's head is."

It's probably not labor, we thought, so we turned off the light and tried to go back to sleep. Five minutes passed. I received another tap.

"It doesn't stop," Kathy told me.

"What doesn't stop?" I asked.

"I don't know."

"Close your eyes, I'm turning on the lights. Let's look at the clock and see if there's any pattern to it. Tell me when something's happening again."

Several minutes pass. "There it is again," Kathy said. "Right now. It's kind of a vague pain down here." She pointed to her lower abdomen, an area where contractions often can first be felt.

I started timing whatever it was I was timing—the vague rumblings Kathy was feeling. Kathy didn't seem to be experiencing the sensations associated with contractions—the wavelike pattern of rising, climax, and fall that occurs fairly rhythmically; 30 . . . 40 . . . 50 seconds went by. Kathy didn't tell me when it ended. "How long does it last?" I asked her again.

"It's better now," Kathy confided. I still had no idea of what to time or whether to time at all. At the childbirth education classes, it was all so nice and orderly. Your wife tells you when the contractions begin, when they end, and you stand by with your watch and note the times. Contractions, we were taught, occur 10 to 15 minutes apart and last 25 to 35 seconds or so in the early stages of labor. They get progressively closer together and stronger, later.

Again, I asked, "Tell me when something starts again." Silence. Kathy's eyes were closed; she was curled up on her side. Maybe she went back to sleep, I thought. Just in case she didn't, I kept my eyes glued to the clock. Three minutes went by.

"It's better now," Kathy stated.

"What's better now?" I asked, becoming more and more anxious. Only three minutes before Kathy had told me the same thing—that it was better now. Didn't our instructor tell us that when contractions are three minutes apart, it meant one was deep into labor, so deep that unless you got to the hospital quickly, you'd better begin preparations for an emergency home delivery? "Could this be active labor?" I wondered. But it's not supposed to come so quickly, without the warning signs we had studied.

"Whatever it is, it's better now," Kathy continued.

"Kathy!" I raised my voice in disbelief. "Kathy, you're in labor and you don't even know it. Good grief! Let's get going."

Remaining quite calm, in sharp contrast to my growing excitement, Kathy was still a bit skeptical. "Let's call the hospital first, just to make sure. I'd hate to call Dr. Hahn at this hour." It was 4:30 A.M. I called the head nurse in the maternity unit who said she thought Kathy was in labor but we'd better call the doctor. "We're reluctant to disturb him at this hour," I told her. Raising her voice, the nurse repeated, "Disturb him? That's what you're paying him for. That's what he's there for."

I called, Kathy talked to him, and he told her to go immediately to the hospital.

The contractions were becoming more intense now—they occurred every 3 to 5 minutes and gradually got stronger and stronger. Kathy indeed was in active labor, having slept through the very early phase. Although outwardly very calm, Kathy was becoming more anxious. "I hope the baby's okay," she said. "I hope everything's okay." I tried to reassure her, telling her how well everything worked out when Kristen was born, that she was in terrific shape, and that things were going to work out just fine.

We began getting ready for the trip to the hospital. We had been advised to have a suitcase packed weeks in advance and to have ready all the items we might need during labor. We were only half prepared. No matter. In a matter of 5 to 10 minutes Kathy and I had gathered together everything we would need—her clothes, various items for the labor kit, the tape recorder with a cassette recording of Aaron Copland's Appalachian Spring and Beethoven's Sixth Symphony.

I called our friends, Milt and Chella Livingston, who had already agreed to come over and take care of our daughter, Kristen, when Kathy was ready to go to the hospital. For months, Kathy and I had spent lots of time with Kristen preparing her for the arrival of the baby. We told her how wonderful it would be when she became a big sister, how she could help take care of her baby brother or sister, and that when the baby got a little older she could have someone to play with and teach him or her all the things she was learning. We also brought Kristen with us when we visited the hospital maternity unit for our preliminary visit. There Kristen met many of the nurses, who made a big hit with her. Kristen was quite excited about the new baby and understood, as best as she could, that Kathy would soon have to go to the hospital for a few days. When I went into Kristen's room to awaken her, I prayed all our careful planning would work. Kristen opened her eyes slowly, wiping them with her hands to get the sand out. "Kristen," I said softly, "Mama's going to have the baby now and we have to go to the hospital. Milt just came over to take you to his house. Chella and Chella Anne are waiting for you." Chella Anne, the Livingston's five-year-old niece, was visiting them that week and she and Kristen had become bosom buddies. Kristen looked around the room, slowly waking up, and then said to me, "Mama's not having the baby now. She's having the baby in July." When Kathy came in the room, followed shortly by Milt, Kristen quickly realized that this indeed must be July. She picked out the clothes that she would wear later in the day, got her favorite tattered blanket, and said she was ready to go. In good spirits, Kristen kissed us all good-bye, telling us she'd come later to visit us at the hospital. Milt picked her up and carried her to his car for the trip back to his home. We were relieved everything went so smoothly—a bit surprised, too, that Kristen didn't even seem a little upset over this unusual departure in the middle of the night. The good planning actually worked: Kristen, who has a very quiet disposition and is secure, knew we would be going soon to the hospital and that she would be staying with our friends. She trusted us and our friends. We were fortunate. Our friends, Milt and Chella, are marvelous with children and are close to Kristen who is their godchild. Kristen looked forward to spending some time with them and did not let a small matter like being awakened in the middle of the night to visit friends bother her.

Before going to the hospital, I called the OB-GYN unit to reserve the birthing room, a hospital room adjoining the labor and delivery rooms. The birthing room is spruced up with curtains and wall hangings and a lounge chair and is used by those who would like to have their babies in a homelike atmosphere. We were in luck. The room was available if we came right away. Like many hospitals across the country, the Lexington County Hospital in West Columbia, South Carolina, where we would be having our child, offered this alternative to those who wished it. For us it would be a welcome change from the traditional, cold, sterile atmosphere of most hospital delivery rooms with their glaring lights, drably colored walls, and strange technological contraptions. We were glad, however, that the delivery room was next door with all its twentieth century paraphenalia, just in case Kathy and the baby needed special assistance should an emergency arise.

I had made arrangements with the admitting clerk at the hospital and with the chief nurse in the maternity unit not to be separated from Kathy on arrival at the hospital and during Kathy's examination and prep procedures. I remembered with regret how we had been separated when Kathy arrived at the hopsital almost four years before to give birth to Kristen: After having driven 38 miles from our home to the hospital, I was ushered into the admissions office to sign papers while Kathy was taken upstairs for an examination in the maternity section. After signing the papers, I rushed upstairs to rejoin Kathy but was told, instead, to wait until she was finished being examined and prepped. I waited for over half an hour in a long, narrow, deserted corridor and grew more and more anxious with every passing minute, afraid something had gone wrong and angry at such a needless separation. When finally I was permitted to join Kathy, who was in active labor, I didn't protest because I didn't want to upset Kathy or make the atmosphere any more tense, but I vowed to myself that when we had other children, I would never let this happen again. I was pleased a few years later during an interview with Elisabeth Bing to hear how strongly she opposed the practice of separation. "There shouldn't be a separation," she said. "The arrival at the hospital is the first real crisis. They take a woman's security blanket away by separating her from her husband." She explained that she felt hospitals create a great deal of dependence on the hospital staff by the expectant parents. Fathers, in particular, are very susceptible to this atmosphere and are too often afraid to insist on not being separated from their wives—both during the admitting process and at other times during labor when they're asked to step out of the room while their wives are examined. "They should say 'No, I will not leave the room,' " concluded Mrs. Bing.

With the birthing room reserved and other arrangements made, Kathy and I arrived at Lexington Hospital at 5:45 A.M. and were promptly escorted to the birthing room. Kathy's labor was progressing much faster than expected, even for a mother who already had one child. A pelvic exam showed her cervix was already dilated to 4 centimeters. This exam, done periodically throughout labor, is one of the most distinct criteria to monitor the progress of labor. A cervix dilated between 4 and 7 centimeters indicates a woman is in the active stage of labor. This stage can last a number of hours, so I began at once assisting Kathy as best I could. As Kathy's contractions got more intense and occurred more frequently—about every 3 minutes—she began using the breathing techniques recommended in our Lamaze class. She took a deep cleansing breath at the start of each contraction, then breathed deeply and slowly throughout the contraction. I helped by timing the contractions, counting off the number of seconds left. This helped Kathy get through one contraction at a time. During the 2 minutes or so between contractions, Kathy lay quietly in a semicollapsed state. I did whatever else I could, wishing only I could do more or, better yet, take on some of the discomfort and pain so it would be easier for her. I freshened wash cloths, which I kept applying to Kathy's forehead. This helped her cool off a bit. I propped up the pillows every time Kathy would change position, I gave her sips of water, I held her hand, I stroked her face and shoulders and arms, and I kept telling her how well she was doing.

About an hour after the first pelvic examination, Kathy was examined again. Her cervix had dilated to approximately 7 centimeters, a clear sign that labor was going so fast the obstetrician was needed in a hurry. At the same time, Kathy was starting to tense up: During each contraction, her fists were tightly clenched and her arms stiffened. She looked immobile and frightened. Her face was dry and pinched in wrinkles, like that of an elderly woman's. I became quite alarmed. I held her hand gently and stroked her arms, reassuring her she was going to be okay, telling her to try to relax. Meanwhile, Joyce Green, the OB-GYN nurse helping Kathy, rushed off to call Dr. James Hahn, our obstetrician. Despite Kathy's efforts to breathe properly during each contraction and my attempts to help her relax, she remained quite rigid and tense. A few minutes later, Joyce returned and said that Dr. Hahn was on his way to the hospital and that he had suggested Kathy take vistaril, a muscle relaxant to relieve the tenseness. We quizzed Joyce carefully about the nature of the medicine, its effects, and how it could affect the baby. After Joyce satisfactorily answered our questions about the medication, Kathy decided to take it. Added to our understanding of the medication was our confidence in Dr. Hahn, whom we already knew prefers his patients to have their children without the assistance of drugs unless it's absolutely necessary. The muscle relaxant worked immediately, giving Kathy much needed relief.

A little after 7:00 A.M., about an hour and a quarter after we had arrived at the hospital, the contractions became so strong that Kathy's legs began shaking almost out of control and she began to moan. I gripped her legs and continued monitoring the special breathing technique she was using—Kathy stayed with the slow, deep breathing recommended for active labor. Again, I felt I wasn't as helpful as I wanted to be, yet I knew that just being there with Kathy, holding her, letting her hear my voice, and monitoring each contraction was important. Although the contractions seemed at this time to be consuming her, Kathy endured them bravely. I was in awe of her strength and courage. Whenever I have heard men who've been with their wives during labor say, "I didn't know my wife had it in her to go through all that. She literally amazed me," I would often wonder if they knew they were being condescending at the same time they offered praise. Watching Kathy in labor, I felt I always knew she had the strength and courage needed to give birth; I was just struck with how she now displayed this strength and courage so dramatically.

At about 7:10 A.M., the contractions were coming every 2 minutes and Kathy's deep, slow breathing just wasn't helping. I had studied and practiced various recommended breathing techniques for each stage of labor and even brought along an excellent little guidebook put out by the Maternity Center Association to consult in a pinch. But in the midst of all the confusion, I forgot which breathing technique to recommend and couldn't spare even a few seconds to look up the chart with the clearly outlined techniques. Fortunately, Joyce Green and the other nurses working with her, all of whom had been offering invaluable assistance throughout the labor, came to Kathy's rescue. They suggested the pant-blow technique, which is helpful in transition. It worked.

At 7:15 the nurses changed shift, and we were introduced to the nurses coming on duty. It was all done quite rapidly and created just a bit more confusion. I overheard Joyce Green tell her replacement, "The doctor's been called and he's on his way." Kathy started having an uncontrollable urge to push. The nurse kept urging Kathy to keep up the pant-blow breathing and not to push. Kathy was in sheer pain—she just about managed to contain the baby, the urge to push was so strong. I asked, "Is Kathy in transition now?" and got the startling reply, "Transition? We're waiting for a doctor. She's well past transition."

We waited a few more minutes. Still no doctor. With each contraction, Kathy began moaning louder and louder. Finally, the nurse assisting Kathy called out to a nurse just entering the room, "We can't wait any longer. We need a doctor now. Go see if there's anyone in delivery who can help!" Then she turned to Kathy and asked, "Is it okay if someone else delivers the baby?" Kathy replied, "I don't care who delivers it. Just get somebody." A substitute doctor was quickly found, and as he was about to put on a surgical gown, in walked Dr. Hahn, with a big smile on his face, clearly delighted he had made it in time. Kathy looked quite pleased to see him. He said a few words to Kathy as he was putting on his gown and then told us, "This is my lucky week. This is the second time this has happened to me this week. Perfect timing." Dr Hahn made a fast assessment of Kathy after getting a report from the nurse. He then began telling Kathy to push, to stop pushing; he tried to avoid giving her an episiotomy but felt there might be unnecessary vaginal tearing in the perineum, so he did a modified episiotomy. I was holding Kathy's hand, watching every move the doctor made, telling Kathy of the baby's progress as its head crowned and began easing through the birth canal. Dr. Hahn gently gripped the baby's smooth, slippery-looking head, still moist from the birth fluids and began turning it. As he did this, he called out, "I think it's going to be a boy, but I'm not sure yet." As the head turned, Dr. Hahn continued pulling. The baby's entire body soon emerged—shoulders, arms, legs. His back was toward us and his entire body was purple, a color one expects since the lungs have not begun to take in oxygen. I shook with excitement, tears running down my face. Kathy, who was propped up with several pillows, strained to get a full view. "Yep," said Dr. Hahn, "I thought so. It's a boy." One of the nurses asked, "What's his name?" Kathy, with the most beautiful smile on her face I had ever seen, looked at me saying "Geoffrey Fiske!" I nodded. "He looks like a Geoffrey," she said. And so we settled on a name. On the way to the hospital we were still undecided as to a name should we have a boy—it was a toss-up between Ian and Geoffrey.

Just as Geoffrey's nose and throat were being cleared by Dr. Hahn, he let out a gentle cry for 5 or 6 seconds. The rush of air filling up his lungs for the first time must have jolted him. Geoffrey was quiet afterward. With his umbilical cord still attached, Geoffrey was placed in Kathy's arms, then covered up with blankets and a tiny skull cap to prevent any loss of heat. In a gentle, high voice, Kathy begin talking to Geoffrey, telling him how beautiful he looked, how happy she was with him. I joined in this chorus of accolades, touching Geoffrey ever so softly, a bit afraid of so precious and fragile a being. A few minutes later, the umbilical cord was cut and Kathy delivered the placenta, thus ending the third and last stage of childbirth. Dr. Hahn carefully examined the placenta, made sure Kathy was still doing okay, and then offered us his warmest congratulations. He said he and the nurses would leave us alone with Geoffrey to get acquainted.

For the next 30 minutes, Kathy and I had the most precious time of our lives with our son. With the lights dimmed and the music of Aaron Copland playing in the background, Geoffrey opened his eyes and, with a little gentle coaxing from Kathy, he began nursing. We talked to him, smiled at him, told him how wonderful he looked, how much we loved him. Kathy was exhausted but in marvelous spirits, a sharp contrast to the dramatic hours before the birth. We were joyful. Geoffrey was healthy, he had ten fingers, ten toes, all that one would expect of a normal, healthy 8-pound, 7-ounce newborn infant and we couldn't have been more thankful and happy and prayerful.

# 8

# Fathers and Newborns

When Bill Kimrey and his wife Penny were expecting their second child, Bill confessed that he hadn't done very much in the area of child care with their first child until the boy was four years old. But now things were different: The social climate had changed and men were generally more aware that they have an important role to play with their newborns. Bill, a high school baseball and basketball coach in South Carolina, wanted to be actively involved with the new baby right from the very beginning. "My son is now six years old," said Bill. "When he was born, I told my wife, 'You take care of him now, and when he's four or five, I'll do everything with him.' I think I missed a lot. I'm close to him now but I think if I'd done more with him earlier I'd have been closer then, too. This time it's going to be different. I want to be close to our child right from the start."

More and more fathers like Bill Kimrey want to begin interacting with their children as soon as they are born. Fortunately, it's much easier to do this today than it was 10 or 20 years ago, when there existed a taboo of sorts against fathers doing much of anything with their newborn infants. Many fathers liked the taboo. Pleading incompetence, they avoided the routine and often messier aspects of infant care. If a father spent any time at all with his newborn, it was usually to play with the baby. There would be more time later to do the things fathers should do with children—when they are old enough to walk and talk. If a father did pitch in by feeding or diapering or walking his newborn in a carriage, his actions were barely tolerated by his male friends and encouraged by no one except his wife. "Twenty years ago when my children were infants," said one early childhood educator and wife of a retired United States Marine colonel, "my husband used to help out all the time. But when some of the men who worked with him came over to the house and saw him changing diapers and feeding the children, they'd tease him and ask, 'What are you doing that for?' "

The anthropologist Margaret Mead once remarked that "No developing society that needs men to leave home and do their 'thing' for the society ever allows young men in to handle or touch their newborns. There's always a taboo against it. For they know somewhere that, if they did, the new fathers would become so 'hooked' that they would never get out and do their 'thing' properly."

So many fathers are openly helping their wives to care for their newborns that the taboo is fast disappearing. It is now socially acceptable for fathers to change diapers, to feed, bathe, cuddle, and play with their infants—to do as much with them as they feel comfortable in doing. What's more, fathers are discovering that by doing more, they indeed are becoming "hooked" on babies. They are discovering the fascination of babies, the unparalleled excitement of watching them grow and develop, the joy of contributing to that process, and the unexpected opportunity to unlock emotions they never knew existed. Bob Miner, author of the widely acclaimed novel *Mother's Day*, was for several years both father and mother to his two small children, one an infant, the other, a toddler. The experience, he said, was profoundly shocking and painful, but ultimately one that opened him up to becoming more deeply human and much closer to his children. Being a full-time father—a mother actually—wrote Miner, "created a rare opportunity for a man, the chance to feel an intimate working part of the lives of my children. Caring for them deepened my emotional repertoire. Breaking and entering as only children can, they ransacked all my closets of deception and defense, making me more vulnerable to the feelings of others and sensitive to their needs, and mine." Mothers, according to Miner, have harbored this secret, refusing even to share it with other mothers, let along fathers.

As more fathers spend more time helping to care for their newborns, they are learning the secrets kept from them for centuries. The leading researchers currently studying fathers are revealing these secrets along with undreamed of truths about fathers and how they can deeply influence their children, beginning at infancy. The three sections that follow will deal with these secrets and truths:

- Knowing the far-reaching findings of the most recent major studies of fathers can help you enormously in understanding and trusting the innate capacity you have to be an effective father.
- Knowing how strong, responsive, capable and totally different each newborn is can help you relate to your infant and be more relaxed with him or her, and also make a significant contribution to your baby's development beginning at birth.
- Knowing the major challenges you and your wife may meet as a result of having a third member in your family can help you take the practical steps needed to enrich this experience.

# About Fathers

There are several fascinating things you should know about fathers that will help you as you become the father of a newborn child.

### Bonding

Fathers can and do bond with their infant children. Until recently, much of the research and writing on bonding ignored this fact and focused mainly on maternal-infant bonding. This is understandable because leading psychologists and theorists, under Freud's influence, have emphasized the mother-infant relationship while ignoring the existence of any father-infant relationship. Freud wrote of "the mother's importance, unique, without parallel, established unalterably for the whole lifetime as the first and strongest love-object, and as the prototype of all later love relations—for both sexes."*

*Sigmund Freud, **An Outline of Psychoanalysis**, Norton, 1949, page 45.

It has been commonly believed that the father-child relationship is most significant later on. The theory was that it is only at the age of three or four that, for the first time, a father's influence is strongly felt—particularly on his child's emerging identity as a boy or a girl and on his or her cognitive and moral development. Current research strongly suggests that a father's influence begins much earlier, that a relationship between him and his child begins during infancy. The first manifestation of this relationship is bonding, which refers to the positive feelings parents first begin having toward their newborn child. Bonding should be clearly distinguished from the concept of the strong bond or relationship that eventually may be established between a parent and his or her child. This bond involves a reciprocal relationship between a parent and his child, is extremely difficult to measure or describe, and may take years and years to establish. According to Dr. Parke, parent-infant bonding represents "the familiarization process, and out of that emerges genuine affection for the baby. Presumably it's going to develop relatively early, and it's going to develop faster if there's more contact."

The bonding or genuine experience of affection toward one's child can begin quite early, especially if a father has early and frequent exposure to his newborn child. But bonding is not instant nor does it occur during any one particular period of time. Referring to the current controversy over whether or not there's a particularly sensitive period immediately after birth when fathers—and mothers—may be more open to bonding, Harvard pediatrician Michael Yogman cautions parents not to overemphasize any one period: "A lot of the debate is about whether there's a particular, salient time period in which it's better for bonding to occur. I'm a little bit skeptical of that because bonding is a dyadic interaction. It's an introduction of two persons, and I think it's the first step in a long process of developing a relationship which is going to go on over a lifetime."

Recent studies have shown, however, that fathers who do witness the birth of their children or are at least exposed to them during the first hours and days after birth generally demonstrate a bonding or enthusiastic attachment to their newborns. They feel strongly that their children are theirs, and they are quite excited about them right from the very earliest contact. One of the most far-reaching studies documenting these responses was done by Dr. Martin Greenberg of San Francisco's Langley Porter Hospital and Dr. Norman Morris of London's Charing Cross Hospital. Enthralled with their newborn infants, the fathers they observed described their infants as beautiful and perfect and said they wanted to spend hours just gazing at them and touching them. These fathers had responses previously associated only with mothers. Other major studies have supported Greenberg and Morris's findings, further contradicting the myth that men are less responsive to newborn children than women are.

Henry Wollman's experience at the recent birth of his daughter Lilly is an example of how responsive fathers can be. His experience is not uncommon. "It was one of the most thrilling experiences of my life," said Wollman.

"All of a sudden, the head was showing and, in a flash, the doctor began rotating her head and easing the rest of her out. Her legs were flopping in the air, and I was anxiously looking to see if she had ten toes and ten fingers. She was perfect. I touched her lightly, afraid she would break under pressure. I was stunned by the beauty of the whole experience."

James Moore of Columbia, South Carolina, presents another example of the strong feelings fathers have when they first meet their newborn children. About the birth of his daughter, Charlotte, Moore felt "an immediate attraction to her, as if there was an instant bond between us. You know, there's a lot of talk about mothers bonding with their babies. But that's true for fathers, too. I felt this closeness with her immediately. It was much quicker than with our first child, Jenny, and I think this was so because this time I was there for labor and delivery. When Jenny was born, I wasn't allowed in for the delivery, although I was there while Georganna was in labor."

Make arrangements beforehand for you and your wife to spend some time alone with your child immediately after the birth. The bonding relationship between you and your child—among all three of you—began before the birth and will grow and develop over a long period of time. Nevertheless, the period after the birth is special for all of you, a time to relax after an intense experience and to enjoy a few quiet moments celebrating the birth—of your baby and of your family—and welcoming your baby.

## Fathers Are Competent

Fathers are just as competent and capable as mothers are of taking care of newborn infants. Most men are brought up with the understanding that they are, through some unexpressed law of nature, not capable of handling babies effectively. This is just not so, contend Ross Parke and other leading researchers who have conducted major studies of fathers and newborns. In one of the first and most important studies of fathers' competence in caring for newborns, Parke and University of Texas developmental psychologist Douglas B. Sawin observed fathers and mothers bottle-feeding their newborn infants, a skill requiring a great deal of sensitivity. To feed newborns successfully one must be able to comfort them when they're anxious, to burp them from time to time when they're in need, and to coax or stimulate them to drink now and again so they will get the amount of milk they need. It is commonly believed that mothers are competent in doing this—it's part of their nature—and fathers are at best clumsy at it and at worst just plain incompetent. Parke and Sawin's study sharply contradicts this common belief. They discovered, surprisingly, that fathers fed their newborns as effectively as the mothers did. Like the mothers, they were competent, capable, and responsive. When the infants fussed during the bottle-feeding sessions, the fathers stopped, tried to determine the problem and dealt with it appropriately by talking to them soothingly, stroking them, or burping them. In a given amount of time, they fed the babies as much milk as the mothers did. Subsequent studies by Parke, Sawin, and other researchers have supported these findings, adding further to a radically new understanding of men as fathers.

Bolstered by the substantial amount of new information about what you are quite naturally capable of doing with your newborn child, you now have a better basis for deciding just how much you *are* going to do. It now is a question of available options, not one of your competence or innate ability.

## How Fathers Interact with Babies

While they can be equally as sensitive to their newborns as mothers are, fathers handle them differently—more vigorously. Mothers handle newborns more smoothly and gently. In one well-known study, Dr. Michael Yogman and his associates at the Boston Children's Hospital Medical Center used two cameras to videotape, separately, the weekly interactions of infants and each of their parents. The sessions, which began when the infants were two weeks old and lasted six months, took two to three minutes and each adult was asked just to play with the infant without using props. The video recordings were analyzed in microscopic detail and showed sharp differences in how fathers and mothers interacted with their infants. "The fathers," said Dr. Yogman, "were more likely to engage in more accentuated rhythmic interchanges, a more physical type of play, and mothers were more likely to engage in more modulated, cycling interchanges—verbal exchanges where the baby coos and the mother imitates the sound."

What this study and others like it reveal is what alert, observant mothers have always known. This is how Georganna Moore of South Carolina described her husband with their three-week-old daughter: "The minute James picks her up, he starts rocking her and talking to her. He feels he's got to be doing something with her. He can't just sit and hold her." Dr. Alison Clarke-Stewart, a University of Chicago developmental psychologist, summarized some of the major differences between the way fathers and mothers handle infants. "If you could separate mothers and fathers into two styles," said Clarke-Stewart, "and it's exaggerated to do so, one could say that the mother's style is talking a lot, and the father's is physical play. Girls are more verbal, more fluent; boys are more physically aggressive—this later gets translated in this rough and tumble play style."

These sharp differences also appear in the ways in which fathers treat male and female infants. Fathers touch, talk, and play more with their firstborn sons than with their firstborn daughters. Fathers—and mothers—perceive their newborn sons differently than their newborn daughters. In a recent major survey, mothers and fathers described their female and male newborns, all of whom were less than 24 hours old, according to the classic male and female stereotypes, even though the newborns did not differ significantly in birth length, weight, or Apgar scores (a physiological assessment of a newborn's responses done immediately after birth). The fathers' descriptions were more extreme regarding differences. To them, newborn boys were seen as stronger, better coordinated, and more alert, while newborn girls were viewed as fragile, delicate, more awkward, and generally weaker. The findings of this and other studies suggests the obvious—that fathers and mothers perceive male and female infants differently and treat them differently. But the obvious is open to serious question. Why, for example, do fathers treat male infants more vigorously than female infants when both are equally as healthy, strong, and responsive? Do fathers handle male infants more vigorously because they grew up with fathers and others who treated them and taught them to play rougher, be tougher, and generally be more aggressive? If male and female babies are inaccurately perceived as different and thus treated accordingly, do they grow up behaving according to the stereotypes associated with men and women because it is expected of them or because it is a part of their nature?

For fathers of newborns, the most provocative immediate question is, Are the differences in how fathers view and treat their male and female infants biologically or culturally based? Dr. Clarke-Stewart found that this is difficult to determine: "Some of it is probably biologically based," she said, "but it's so hard to separate cultural and biological differences when the social condition supports something that might be instinctual."

Some of the most exciting studies of fathers and infants are suggesting that cultural influences have been labeled as biological. In a study she did of fathers who stay at home and take care of their infants while their wives work, University of Miami research psychologist Dr. Tiffany Field found that these fathers interacted with their infants as do mothers who stay at home with their infants. Like the mothers, these men smiled at and imitated their infants more than do fathers who do not take care of their children full time, and they talked to them in the high-pitched tones often associated with mothers. "The only interpretation I could make of this," explained Dr. Field, "was that fathers who had more experience with their babies, or who were more familiar with the babies than their wives were, learned more quickly some of the things babies enjoyed doing. I started out thinking fathers and mothers were innately different in the way they relate to babies, but what I found suggested that the differences were more a function of exposure and familiarity."

What is so exciting about this conclusion and the results of other studies of fathers is that you do not have to be locked into a stereotypic pattern. You can be the kind of father you feel comfortable in being, and you can make a significant contribution to helping your newborn child grow up without the limitations imposed by rigid, traditional sex roles.

As more fathers spend more time with their infants, will their treatment of boys versus girls also evolve into something more responsive to the infant instead of to cultural stereotypes? Yes, said Ross Parke. "The way fathers interact with boys and girls is culturally based and has nothing to do with either girls or boys—or fathers necessarily—and I expect it will change as the stereotyped roles for mothers and fathers change."

## Fathers, the Forgotten Contributors to Infant Development

The fourth, and most important recent discovery about fathers, is that they do make a difference to infants. They are no longer, to quote University of Michigan developmental psychologist Dr. Michael Lamb, "the forgotten contributors to child development."

A father's contribution during the early weeks and months is first reflected in the infant's recognition of his active presence. As early as three or four weeks, the baby may respond to his or her father slightly differently than to the mother. Dr. Michael Yogman tells of a three-week-old girl in one of his studies who was lying in an upright infant seat. Slumped over and looking sleepy, she became suddenly quite alert when her father started playing with her, engaging her through a tapping game with his fingers gently touching her face. She gave just the slightest whisp of a smile, indicating that not only did she recognize him but she expected a slightly different behavior from him than from her mother, whom she responded to warmly but less dramatically. Subsequent encounters over six months supported the interpretation of this very early pattern regarding this infant's response to her father.

When an infant is older, the effects of his father's relationship to him, as it has been established in the early days and weeks, is more clearly demonstrable. "Some of the data from studies of infants from eight months to a year," said Dr. Parke, "indicate that if fathers are more involved, the infants are going to test higher, they are going to be more socially responsive, and generally they are going to be able to withstand stressful situations better." Dr. Frank Pedersen of the National Institute of Child Health and Human Development, suggested in a study of five- to six-month-old infants that the more active their fathers were with them, the higher they scored on the Bayley Mental Development Index, a test that measures infants' cognitive and motor skills. These findings are supported by the results obtained by Dr. Milton Kotelchuck, a developmental psychologist who is director of health statistics and research for the Commonwealth of Massachusetts, and several of his colleagues. They have shown, in a series of four studies of 300 infants from six to 24 months old, that infants whose fathers frequently bathed and dressed them withstood stress better than infants whose fathers didn't do as many of these caretaking tasks.

There is also evidence that fathers have a significant indirect effect on their infants' cognitive and social development. A father who applauds each new thing his baby masters reinforces the baby—and also encourages the mother to continue teaching the baby. In a far-reaching study of this complex pattern, Alison Clarke-Stewart concluded, "If fathers interacted more actively with their babies, it seemed to influence the mothers to spend more time stimulating their babies and that was what had a positive effect on them."

Whether direct or indirect, fathers indeed are no longer the forgotten contributors to infant development. Said Dr. Yogman, "Fathers are special, and they do have a direct and unique role to play with their babies right from the very beginning."

# About Newborns

Like the image of fathers, the image of newborns is slowly but finally changing, making it possible for fathers to discover what observant mothers have known all along: that infants are highly competent, capable, and responsive. The American philosopher William James once described the early infancy period with the words "bloomin', buzzing confusion," a description that reflected a popular image of infants that has only begun to change during the last 20 years.

Consider the circumstances that surrounded the birth of an infant 20 years ago and the circumstances today. Until fairly recently, when a baby was born in a hospital, he was quickly examined, his ears and throat were cleared, he was dried off, given eye drops, bundled up, briefly shown to his mother if she wasn't still affected by the anesthesia, and rushed off to the nursery to be carefully observed and monitored. Often the baby would be affected by the drugs administered to his mother in labor as well as the loss of energy experienced during the journey through the birth canal. As a result, he'd immediately fall into a deep sleep for as much as six or seven hours. During the first 24 hours, his mother was generally prohibited from touching him, and so he was fed, cuddled, and diapered by the nursery staff which acted as surrogate mothers. If the mother was feeling up to it, she—along with her husband—could see the baby through the glass window of the nursery later during the day. This commonly accepted set of practices in hospitals reinforced the notion that newborns were unresponsive during their early hours and days. These practices, in addition, reflected a common failure to recognize the critical importance of early contact between parents and child. The newborn infant was segregated unnecessarily not only from his father, but from his mother as well. This was particularly unfortunate because the total separation interfered with the natural transition from life inside the womb to life outside of it. It was not known, or was too often forgotten, that the infant is as dependent on his mother immediately after birth as he was before, even though his life-support system now functions independently. Nine months in the womb constitute only the first stage of a newborn's development, only part of the period of gestation; the first few months after birth constitute a continuation of this period.

Circumstances surrounding the birth of a baby today are very different from those of the traditional hospital delivery. In most progressive hospitals and maternity centers, frequent and early contact of mother and child and of father and child is encouraged, especially during the period immediately following birth. Current research findings of studies of newborns during this early period have strongly influenced promotion of this early contact. The research is demonstrating what mothers and fathers discover about newborns after birth. A newborn is surprisingly responsive. He is most probably fatigued, given the arduous journey through the birth canal, yet he can be alert and responsive for as much as 30 to 45 minutes after birth, before he falls asleep. During this first period the baby can let out a healthy cry as his lungs fill up with air for the first time and as he encounters the cool air outside the warm, safe, dark, weightless environment of the womb. He also can hear fairly well, distinguishing high-pitched sounds; and in the comforting arms of his mother, he can turn his head in the direction of the characteristically high-pitched tone of her voice. His eyes are very sensitive to bright lights, and they will be for some time; but when the lights of the room are dimmed, the baby will open his eyes and move them back and forth as he records his first images. He indeed can see and respond to the visual objects before him. Since touch, the primary sense, is the one that dominated his existence in the womb, he is most responsive to it at birth. After all, he's been floating for nine months in the warm, soothing birth fluids. So when he rests on his mother's bare stomach, supported by her arms and caressed by her, he responds to this enveloping exposure to touch with contentment.

A newborn is also stronger than has been commonly believed. He has relatively great strength in his hands—his tight grasp, for example, is estimated to have about 2 pounds of pulling power.

With a little coaxing and a guiding embrace, the baby can begin to nurse. The nursing releases maternal hormones that further hasten uterine contractions, thus more quickly reducing the size of the uterus and reducing bleeding. The newborn receives colostrum from his mother's breasts, a thin, sticky, colorless fluid that nourishes him as well as clears his intestines and provides immunity against some diseases. Within 72 hours, his mother's milk will begin coming in. After being awake, sometimes for as long as 45 minutes, the baby will fall into a deep sleep that could last six or seven hours, a sleep needed to restore the energy he expended during the birth process.

What's more remarkable than a newborn's activity immediately after birth is that each newborn responds in a different manner, reflecting his individual temperament. Harvard pediatrician T. Berry Brazelton talks about the quiet baby, the average baby, and the active baby in describing an infant's basic temperament. Sometimes during the first minutes after birth, a baby's responses will foretell whether he'll be active or average or quiet. Less than two minutes after our son Geoffrey was born, our obstetrician told us, "I think he's going to be a very calm baby." Amazed that he could make such a prediction so early, Kathy and I decided to wait and see. Months later, we recalled his remark and, sure enough, he had been right. Geoffrey was a very calm or quiet baby with a very easy-going, even temperament. Some of our friends referred to him as a "good" baby, a term used to distinguish a quiet or calm baby from one whose temperament is more active. "Good" used this way is an unfortunate term, because it implies that if a baby is more active and perhaps more fretful at times, he is not a "good" baby but a "bad" baby. This implication is absurd, given the innocent, vulnerable, and dependent state of all infants. Thus the descriptive accounts of babies as being quiet, average, or active, which can be observed early on, is a better way of viewing them.

During the first six weeks, the newborn is in the first phase of his development outside the womb, a period of adjustment to the radical changes occurring to him. He gradually begins to see more clearly, to recognize sounds better, and to gain strength. As each day passes, he will be awake more and more. If one computed the average amount of time the newborn is alert during the day, it would read like this: three minutes per hour the first week, up to five minutes per hour around the fourth week, and at eight to ten weeks, he will be alert approximately 15 minutes an hour during the day.

While he slowly but steadily grows stronger and becomes more alert, the most dramatic and noticeable development—at least from a father's and mother's perspective—occurs when he's about six to eight weeks old. That development is the social smile—he begins to smile more frequently in response to your words and gestures. Parents get faint glimpses of this earlier, but it is stronger and clearly noticeable now. Another dramatic development that until recently has never been widely observed, occurs between the fourth and eighth or ninth week. An infant can discern differences in the sounds and voices of his parents, and may react differently, though this is difficult to perceive immediately, in response to his father's and mother's voices.

## About Fathers, Mothers, and Newborns

What you learn from this and other books and what you learn from childbirth education classes, parent groups, and discussions with other parents will help you become a well-informed, active father of a newborn. What will help you, above all else, is to learn to trust your deepest instincts and to act on them. During the hectic transition from being a husband to being a husband and a father, catch your breath from time to time and take time to reflect on what and how you're doing. Discuss pressing concerns—about the baby, about yourselves—with your wife, read and evaluate critically what you read, and then, finally, decide for yourself what and how much you feel you should do as a new father.

In learning to trust your feelings more, bear in mind that in all you do for and with your baby, you should try to see what he must be experiencing from his point of view. Remember, your baby is encountering almost overwhelming physiological and psychological changes in a time when he is most vulnerable, and during which he is totally dependent on others. Don't forget that he is totally innocent, entirely incapable of doing anything to offend, and that it is virtually impossible to spoil him during the months of his early infancy. Remember, too, that he is quite capable and, despite his vulnerable circumstances, he expresses himself as effectively as he can, showing discomfort through crying and fussing and pleasure by smiling or just displaying a quiet contentment.

By being sensitive to his circumstances, knowing as much as you can about a newborn and knowing how difficult it must be to make sense out of so many changes all at once, you will be able to be empathetic toward him, one of the most important qualities in being an effective father. This will serve you well during the times when you and your wife may have been up all night with your newborn who's been having great difficulty settling down, and you are at your wit's end trying to find some way to console him. If this occurs during the first day or so home from the hospital, remember that your newborn is having a tough time making the adjustment to his new mode of existence. This knowledge may help you make it through the night without losing your cool or without directing your anger and frustrations toward the other person nearest you—your wife—who is probably as frustrated and upset as you are.

## Interacting with Your Newborn

What can you do to be actively involved with your newborn child? First, you can make sure that well before the birth you arrange to have early and frequent contact with your infant during his first hours and days. Try to spend at least 5 to 15 or 20 minutes quietly with your newborn immediately after his birth. This will help promote a feeling of closeness or bonding with him for both you and your wife. Touch your newborn freely but gently. This is one of the most effective ways of reducing any fears you may have of handling such a precious, innocent, and vulnerable being. Look him in the eyes: Direct contact gives you a more dramatic sense of his individual identity. Talk to him—softly, gently, naturally. He may not be able to understand your words but he does hear what you are saying and he responds to you in a very subtle and rhythmic way through his barely discernible movements. This manner of responding to you is contagious: If you're open to it, you will soon be hooked on your newborn. This period immediately after birth is indeed very special.

Richard McCoy's experience with his daughter after her birth is an example of what frequently happens. Richard and his wife Marsha knew it was important to have some time alone with their child after the birth, so they made the necessary arrangements with their obstetrician. "It was a sacred time," said Richard. "The lights in the delivery room had been dimmed and voices were lowered, creating a peaceful atmosphere. After the baby emerged from the birth canal, she was placed on Marsha's bare stomach to rest and get acquainted with her new parents. The delivery room staff then left the room. For 20 minutes Richard and Marsha talked gently to Kate, stroked her, cuddled her, and gazed in her eyes before Kate fell into a deep sleep in Marsha's arms. After this period of bonding Richard and Marsha immediately felt a strong sense of attachment to Kate.

Try especially during those first hours and days to become very familiar with your newborn child. Learn the skills you'll need to be comfortable in caring for him. If possible, arrange to take a week or so from work to spend that time with your baby and your wife. The more you learn and do, the closer you'll be to both of them. And if you acquire the skills quickly, if possible right at the hospital, you will avoid problems that often arise during the first days the baby is home.

## First Days at Home

Too often, new parents describe the baby and mother's first days at home as "hellish." One of the reasons these days can be "hellish" is that the parents have not been permitted to spend enough time with their newborn at the hospital. As a result, they don't learn the skills they need and they leave the hospital lacking confidence in their ability to care for their baby. Even if a mother received some type of instruction at the hospital, there is another problem: Fathers often feel left out. "You set up a discrepancy," said Dr. Parke, "if you have the mother involved in the hospital and the father excluded. When the parents get home, you immediately have a discrepancy in terms of who is better acquainted with the baby, who feels more confident, who's had practice implementing the kinds of skills necessary for early care of the baby."

To get to know your infant better, get involved right from the start. When he's in the room with you and your wife, help take care of him. The more experience you gain in the hospital, the better it will be during the first days home. Take advantage of the maternity staff: They enjoy caring for babies, are skilled at it, and are more than willing to assist you in learning what you need to know. But don't let them take over or you'll leave the hospital without the practical skills you need to care for the baby.

Many hospitals offer informal classes in child care to small groups of mothers in the maternity section. The classes cover how to feed, diaper, and bathe babies. They also try to teach how to interpret and respond to the cues babies give about being hungry, uncomfortable, or in need of extra affection. If these classes are open to fathers, attend them. If they are not available or are held at inconvenient times for you, take time during your visits to have your wife teach you what she has learned. Although she may possibly be doing most of the child care, you are both coparents ultimately responsible for your child; therefore, you will be more effective as a father if you know what you're doing. You'll be able to offer your wife welcome relief on evenings and weekends, so she can get away from time to time. She needs these periods of rest; she also needs to know that you are competent to care for your infant, that she doesn't have to take on all the burden and responsibility. After all, it took two to conceive the baby, and it should follow that two also share in caring for the baby within the framework of the roles each plays.

At the hospital, learn, for starters, how to change a diaper, but don't be put off by a little screaming at first, whether it's you who does the screaming or your baby. Fathers—and mothers for that matter—tend to be a bit nervous when they start changing diapers. In fact, fathers and mothers alike are usually somewhat apprehensive at first about handling newborns, especially if they've never been around babies before. Studies have shown that mothers, contrary to myths about their instinctual habits, have to learn the skills needed to care for babies just as fathers do. Everyone thinks this knowledge comes naturally to mothers. It doesn't. Mothers just learn to care for babies fast because their babies would go hungry and neglected if they didn't; in the process of learning they get over some of their fears. Fathers have had a "choice," claiming it is not part of their nature or role to handle babies. But once you've changed a few diapers and become less self-conscious about it, you'll discover there's more to changing a diaper than merely keeping a baby dry. The few minutes it takes can be a special time to pause a bit and converse with your baby—bent over him you have a marvelous position for great eye-to-eye contact (if you have a boy don't bend over too much or you may on occasion get sprayed, so keep a diaper handy for safety's sake). During diaper time, you have an excellent opportunity to interact with him, to watch more closely how he responds to you. Sometimes during the first few days home, he may not respond so positively during diaper changes, but this soon changes when the process becomes routine for him. Once you become skilled at diaper changing, you'll be more relaxed, and your infant will be equally relaxed, making the task a lot less onerous than it is sometimes made out to be. Once, when I was leaning over changing my son Geoffrey's diaper on the floor in a remote corner of a library, a man smiled down on me and said: "I've somehow always managed to avoid doing that. I have a son who's 17 months old and we're expecting another one soon." He laughed and asked me how I "got stuck" taking my son to the library with me. I didn't get stuck, I told him, explaining that my wife and I worked together at taking care of our children. Later, I thought, this man doesn't even know what he's missing—not the changing of diapers, which can be messy at times, but the thousands of opportunities to spend a few minutes with one's child, holding him, soothing him, talking to him, and playing with him, opportunities that cement a strong relationship with the child for a lifetime.

Learn how to bottle-feed your infant if your wife has chosen not to nurse him. Even if she is nursing, the pediatrician may recommend a supplemental or replacement bottle feeding of a formula or of water every evening in order to give your wife a rest and to give you the opportunity to share in the feeding. Learn also to bathe him, although you probably won't start doing this until he returns home from the hospital. When you do start, try doing it together with your wife. Later, do it by yourself. Some fathers believe this is the most enjoyable and exciting time they have with their newborns.

Learn, too, what cues your baby routinely gives and how to respond to them. Again, keep in mind that it is virtually impossible to spoil an infant, something that can be forgotten when he becomes very demanding. Remember, he's at a very vulnerable stage, and one of the most important things for him to develop is a sense of trust. It's important, therefore, to give him all the affection and attention you can. If he cries excessively, there is often a good reason for it. Infants, it should be noted, should never be allowed to "cry it out," although there are times when some crying cannot be avoided and must be accepted. But crying for close to an hour or more would represent an extreme that should be avoided.

Some things to be on the alert for: Infants have very sensitive skin, which is easily irritated when their diapers are soaked. If this is the problem, change the diaper. If he's hungry, feed him or have your wife feed him if she's nursing him. During the first days or sometimes week or so at home, while he is adjusting to his new environment, he may need to eat more often—every two hours or so until his system adapts. Be careful not to think of your infant as an empty hot water bottle that must constantly be filled with food. Being hungry is not the only reason he may become cranky, and food is not a cure-all for crankiness. Sometimes an infant may just be in a fretful mood, just as you may at times be in a fretful mood. At those times, after you've tried to console him, there's nothing more you can do. But consider other possibilities before you give up trying to help. Your newborn might be irritable because he's just plain uncomfortable. He might also be bored—yes, bored. He doesn't have to be entertained all the time, but there are times when he sits too long or is in one place too long and he gets bored. Consider how bored you might become if you saw everything in your house while stretched out on a quilt in your living room or confined in a small patch of grass with bars closing you in. The Russians, well aware of this problem, use cribs that can be raised several feet off the floor so their babies can see better what's happening around them—they then see everything in the room, including their parents, at the level at which you see everything. It's an ingenious idea because it helps prevent babies from getting bored with the limited view they have when they spend so much time on the floor level.

Newborns are easily disturbed and frequently need lots of comforting. Some pediatricians recommend that newborns not see too many different people during their first week home, in order to avoid confusing them with so many new faces—they need the time to get acquainted with their parents. They will cry easily and loudly when they're moved abruptly or when they hear loud noises. Usually they regain their composure rather quickly, although there may be times when nothing seems to console them—neither being cuddled nor rocked nor fed. Sometimes it just takes them a little longer to calm down. Rocking is frequently a very effective way of calming infants. If your newborn seems to be totally out of control and you've tried everything imaginable, take him for a drive—it works miracles. Strap the baby safely and securely in an infant car seat, place him in your car, buckle the infant seat up with a safety belt, and just drive around. This ultimate method is recommended by many doctors and by parents who've tried it in moments of desperation.

There's a striking response you may notice in your infant when he hears a loud noise or when he sees very bright lights—the startle or Moro reflex.

He will actually be startled and respond by throwing up his hands and arms as if he were about to lead a 20-piece orchestra. This is a normal response and you should not be alarmed by it. If he doesn't quickly settle down afterward, sometimes placing your hand firmly on his chest and stomach will short-circuit, so to speak, the startle reflex and calm him.

## At Home with the Baby

My wife Kathy and I had very little experience with babies before our daughter Kristen was born. As a teenager, Kathy babysat for some of her neighbors' young children, and in an emergency I once babysat for some children of a friend. It was then that I changed a diaper for the first time. As I recall, I did it quite awkwardly and with some trepidation. The child, a 10-month-old girl, sensed my fear of the whole process and wailed uncontrollably, making me from that moment on marvel at the speed, skill, and poise of those who can change diapers so effortlessly.

At the Vermont hospital where Kristen was born, Kathy attended some informal classes on caring for babies. I wasn't able to go to any of these, so I had to learn as much as I could from Kathy, although during the visits to the hospital after Kristen's birth, I got the chance to change a few diapers. Fortunately, I was less anxious and Kristen was very cooperative.

Even after three days at the hospital, Kathy hadn't had enough opportunity to learn all the skills she needed to feel abundantly competent in caring for a newborn. I didn't have as much exposure to Kristen as I would have liked to have had, so at that time I never even dreamed I could or should be skilled in caring for a newborn. Since I was relying on Kathy and the skills she was supposed to have as a mother, I left the hospital knowing next to nothing about how to care for a baby. Both Kathy and I were apprehensive about our new responsibilities as parents. Our anxiety could be seen easily the morning we left the hospital with Kristen. A very solicitous nurse helped us carry Kristen to our car for the 38-mile ride to our home in Waterville, Vermont. So nervous were we, that getting Kristen into our Volkswagon with all her gear and securing her safely in her new baby seat was done with more fanfare than accorded chiefs of state.

Kristen loved all the attention, or so it seemed, and enjoyed the ride home—at least she appeared contented because she slept most of the way. I thought she was relaxed because I drove so slowly and cautiously. Actually, infants really do enjoy car rides. It was years later that I learned how car rides can be the most effective way of calming hysterical infants. I wish I had known that later during our first day home with Kristen.

We arrived home at noon and were greeted by Kathy's mother Peggy and Kathy's sister Linda. They were visiting us for three or four days to help out. For the rest of the day, Kristen was in rather good form: She slept a lot and generally seemed content. Shortly after midnight, however, she started crying and just wouldn't stop. Kathy nursed her, rocked her in her arms, paced the floor with her, but all her efforts to calm Kristen were unsuccessful. I tried my hand at consoling her but everything I did failed. Kristen was inconsolable. After trying literally everything we could, we finally brought Kristen to bed with us. There Kathy held Kristen in her arms, rocking her gently, while I held Dr. Spock—his book on child care—and frantically thumbed through its pages to find out what was wrong with Kristen and what we could do about it. I read passages aloud to Kathy, which only made matters worse because we began thinking Kristen had symptoms for everything that's ever been known to happen to infants. Every 15 minutes or so, we'd trade: I'd hold Kristen while Kathy held Dr. Spock. Just as we were thinking the worst, Kristen would calm down for a few minutes and we would quietly try putting her back in her crib. Then she'd start fussing again. This continued through the night. Every hour or so, Kathy's mother and sister would come to our room to make suggestions and try their hand at calming Kristen. But even Peggy, who successfully raised three daughters, wasn't able to console her. At daybreak, Kristen at last quieted down and went off to sleep for four precious hours.

Kristen's second day at home was much more peaceful. By the third day, she adjusted to her new home and to her new parents fairly well. Or, to put it more accurately, we adjusted to Kristen. We began feeling comfortable with her and she responded accordingly.

One of the problems we faced that first day home with Kristen is common to many new parents. We didn't know anything about babies, and we felt nervous taking care of Kristen. I believe Kristen sensed this anxiety. If you and your wife can spend enough time with your newborn at the hospital (if possible, four or more hours a day), your first days at home with him may be relatively calm and not necessarily "hellish." The infant's constant needs may exhaust you, but you will have had the time to get to know him and be very much at ease with him. This confidence will make things go more smoothly.

Before your baby is born, try to spend some time with a friend or neighbor's baby. Hold the baby and learn what they do in caring for him. Talk to them about their first experience as parents. What was it like when they came from the hospital with their baby? They may have valuable suggestions and can offer you encouragement. Just watching a baby, holding him, and changing his diaper may help reduce your anxiety about taking care of your own baby.

Kathy's mother Peggy stayed with us for four days and she was a godsend. While I went off to work each day, she advised Kathy about caring for Kristen, and she and Kathy's sister Linda cooked and took care of the house while Kathy devoted all her time to Kristen. It was only much later that I realized the need for me to have been there with Kristen and Kathy during those first days—I felt I missed something by not being there. When our son Geoffrey was born four years later, I was home during the first weeks and was thrilled to spend the time getting to know him and sharing in caring for him.

It is very helpful to be there with your wife, at least during the first week. If you can't be home, arrange to have someone else spend time with your wife during those first days with the baby. If someone can come to help and both of you can be there, so much the better. Both of you need to be freed of household duties for a while, so you can concentrate on the task of learning to care for your baby and, more importantly, on getting to know your baby. If someone comes to help, make it clear beforehand that you and your wife are in charge of your baby but that you definitely need and want their valued advice. This done, you will avoid any possible misunderstandings later. Said one new father who didn't arrange beforehand to let his mother-in-law know that he was going to play an active role in caring for his newborn child: "I didn't mind it very much—actually it was funny. But every time I picked up my daughter the first day she was home from the hospital, my mother-in-law, who was staying with us to help, would say to me, 'Do you want me to take her?' and then she would rush over and whisk her away from me."

If you don't have anyone to spend some time with you and your wife, take over running the house yourself—cooking meals, cleaning, running errands. Even though you will want to spend as much time with your newborn as possible, you have to consider your wife's situation. She will more than likely still be exhausted from giving birth and adjusting to her new schedule and probably feels somewhat confined. Lack of sleep, which is not uncommon during the first days or even weeks, may make matters even worse at times. So if you can free her of some of the household duties, she will be able to regain her strength faster and concentrate on caring for the baby. Sharing in the care of the baby is another important way of helping your wife as she makes the readjustment after birth.

## Baby Blues

Your wife may experience a period of sadness or "postpartum blues" during the third or fourth day or so after she gives birth. "About a week after my daughter was born," said one mother from South Carolina, "I was taking a bath and glanced down at my stomach and was overcome with sadness. I had such a feeling of emptiness, like I had lost something precious." This sadness may pass quickly or it may last several weeks.

It is still unknown what precisely causes postpartum blues, but one contributing factor may be that a mother doesn't see her baby enough during the first few days after his birth. A major factor is the tremendous emphasis placed on the climactic moment of the birth itself by the mother and father, by their friends, and especially by those involved in preparing them for the birth. So much emphasis is placed on the birth that what follows the birth is many times ignored—what do you do with the baby after he's born, what kinds of problems one might encounter afterward, what are the major challenges to a mother and father, and how do you prepare for the changes you are going to have to make. A mother has been anxiously awaiting the birth of her child for nine months, but immediately after his birth, the child is whisked away from her, and she may not see him very much during the critical first few days. In addition, she may not see her husband very often, either, if the hospital has rigid restrictions about visiting hours. She also may not be able to see any of her close friends or relatives. What may contribute the most to the blues, however, is that during the short periods when she does see the baby, she may not be permitted to take charge of him. Hospital staff members, with admittedly good intentions, may take over for her, thus hampering the mother in getting the experience and skills she needs to take care of her baby. Other contributing factors to postpartum depression may be the hormonal imbalance in a woman's body and the new demands of motherhood.

If your wife is going through postpartum blues or feeling a bit sad after she gives birth, offer her lots of extra support. One effective way to do this is by taking care of household matters or fully sharing in caring for the baby—changing diapers, feeding him, taking him for walks in the baby carriage. Above all, be sensitive to her feelings. She may have very deep and conflicting feelings during this dramatic transition, and so may you. You may feel resentment toward the baby for disrupting your lives, for interfering with your freedom. These feelings most often exist alongside deep feelings of affection and love for the baby. The negative feelings are disturbing in particular because your wife probably has been brought up with the notion that mothers should only have sweet and loving feelings toward their children. Remember that it is quite natural for her to experience moments of deep resentment toward the baby, toward you, and toward herself. Fortunately, they are moments only, and in a short period of time these moments usually pass.

## Communication

Be sensitive to the possible existence of these tense moments and encourage your wife to talk about them. You, in turn, aren't immune from them yourself, so talk freely to her about your feelings. But most important of all, accent the positive: Encourage your wife, ask her about her deepest positive feelings toward the baby, tell her you love her, and just be there for her. Unfortunately, a great deal of needless suffering goes on because mothers and fathers are ashamed to express feelings they have that seem so "unmotherly" or "unfatherly." Dr. Philip A. Cowan, a psychologist at the University of California at Berkeley, said that being open and honest with each other about their feelings is crucial for parents of newborn infants. Communication is the key to an effective transition from couple to family.

Because you face such a dramatic transition so quickly, it is not only crucial that you and your wife talk freely and openly with each other but that you also talk openly with your close friends. Those who have children can be extremely helpful and supportive, because they've faced the challenges you are facing now. Dr. Cowan has found that new parents can also find encouragement and support in talking with other new parents, perhaps in a group setting. "A group is helpful because it makes couples set aside from a few minutes to two hours during the week to talk about issues when they're not angry or upset. Also, when you get a group of four couples in a room to talk about how they do things, how they work out their roles, and how they communicate with each other, they begin to see that there are many different ways of doing things." However helpful groups are, though, Dr. Cowan does not feel they are necessary as long as a husband and wife can openly and calmly discuss the problems they are experiencing.

In many communities across the country, women who have sensed the need for new mothers to be in touch with other mothers have established informal groups, many sponsored by childbirth education groups. In these groups, new mothers meet regularly and give and share the support they need in facing the challenges of their new roles as mothers.

Elisabeth Bing, renowned childbirth educator, is an advocate of such groups. In each of her classes, Mrs. Bing urges expectant mothers to get to know one another and to exchange phone numbers. "These numbers serve as a hotline, a number to call before you get so overwhelmed you feel like flushing the baby down the toilet—if you haven't had any sleep in 48 hours, and you just can't take it anymore, and you need someone to talk to who understands."

You may need to talk to others, too, especially to fathers who can offer you their support. Until recently, fathers have almost exclusively played the role of breadwinners, leaving the task of caring for very young children to their wives. The general culture hasn't strongly supported fathers who want to share as much as they can in the actual day to day care of their young children and become physically and emotionally close to them. If you wish to play a more active role, find some allies and discuss everything from what they actually do as fathers to why they do it. If you don't know any fathers, make it a point to meet some in your childbirth education classes. In most cases, these expectant fathers have come to the classes because they want to be actively involved with their children. Sharing your experiences with one another as you embark on the exciting adventure of becoming fathers may prove very rewarding.

## Defining Your Role

Decide what kind of role you're going to play as a father of your newborn child before he's born. Planning ahead like this will help you and your wife make an easier transition during the early weeks and months after the birth. In a major study he did of expectant fathers, Harvard psychologist Dr. Robert Fein found that fathers and mothers who sat down with one another before their child's birth and determined the role each was to play once the baby was born made relatively easy postpartum adjustments. This was true of fathers who decided to play traditional roles and of fathers who decided to play more active ones. "If a couple basically decided that they were going to see parenting as a two-person experience," said Dr. Fein, "they tended to do that before the birth of the child and after it. The men developed fathering roles beforehand that included being actively involved in taking care of their newborn children."

During the pregnancy period, therefore, it is important that you and your wife discuss and raise many questions about your roles and decide, as best you can, what they will be. Is your wife going to return to work? If so, will she be working full time or part time? When will she return? If both of you are going to work, will you share 50/50 in caring for your baby when you are together at home? Often when both parents work full time, the mother, when she's home, still does most of the child care. If she does this while working full time, she may become very resentful. This can cause much friction, so if you and your wife are both employed, be sensitive to possible problems in this area.

If your wife decides to take a more traditional role and stay home to care for the baby, how much are you going to share in that care evenings after work and on weekends? One mother, whose husband worked while she stayed home with the baby, was worried he would feel left out because she was spending so much time nursing their daughter. She was afraid he wouldn't have a chance to do much with her until after she stopped nursing her. So she and her husband figured out a way for him to better share in caring for her. For each of the feedings at night, he would bring the baby to his wife, then he'd spend that time with them. Afterward, he would help burp her, change her diaper, and play with her. He made sure that he'd spend at least one or two hours each night with his daughter—not just by being in the same room with her but by actively interacting with her. On weekends, he would take over for his wife for four or five hours so she could have some time for herself. The rest of the time, the three of them would spend together.

For many new fathers whose wives are home full time caring for the baby, the idea that a mother needs time to herself seems almost incomprehensible. "What *do* you do all day?" is a familiar question asked by many men as they return from work and find that the baby has been well cared for but all kinds of household chores have been neglected. "Doesn't the baby sleep most of the day?" these fathers may wonder. The truth is that being solely responsible for your baby's care day in and day out is at the same time rewarding and physically and mentally taxing. One needs a clean break from time to time to be by oneself, even if it's only for an hour or two.

For a deeper appreciation of this need, spend one or two days in complete charge of caring for the baby—complete: diapers, feeding, bathing, soothing, naps, cleaning, and the morning and afternoon outing with the carriage. Do one or two errands with the baby at your side—shopping for groceries, for example, or a trip to the cleaner's—and then prepare one or two meals, answer the phone four or five times, call a serviceman for an appointment to fix an appliance, do two loads of laundry, empty the trash, and take care of the five or six other chores one might do in a typical day at home. As beautiful and loving as your baby can be at various times throughout the day, you'll quickly realize why your wife needs some time for herself, especially if before the baby's birth she was working outside the home and sharing all the household chores with you.

Another area to consider before the baby is born is how restricted are you going to become because you have a newborn child. "I can't wait for the baby to be born," said one expectant father, "but I'm afraid we're going to have a lot less freedom." This father voiced a common fear many new parents have. It is true, major adjustments have to be made. You are going to be restricted to a certain extent, but if you understand how to care effectively for your infant and plan well, the restrictions on your freedom are not as major as people frequently fear they will be. Although you will have to make some trade-offs, the advantages and excitement of being a father far outweigh any disadvantages.

The fear of being severely restricted in where you can go and even in having people come visit you can be particularly troublesome the first week your infant is home from the hospital. A few days after they brought their newborn daughter Kate home from the hospital, Richard and Marsha McCoy invited some friends over for dinner. Richard and Marsha were still uncomfortable about their new role as parents, but their daughter seemed to be doing well and they looked forward to a quiet evening with their friends. Kate had other plans. She cried the entire evening and was inconsolable. When their friends finally left, said Richard, "Marsha and I thought we would never again be able to have friends over, let alone ever go out anywhere. We were depressed." It took Richard and Marsha two weeks before things calmed down and they discovered they were indeed able to go out fairly frequently and that they could have friends over regularly. What happened was that they were gaining confidence and expertise taking care of Kate, and Kate was making the adjustments she needed to make during those early weeks of her life. Her parents did what so many others tend to do during stressful moments—they absolutized—saw the bleak condition of a particular moment as permanent.

Once you discover how quickly your newborn adjusts, you won't feel so restricted. Newborns actually sleep most of the time and can sleep almost anywhere. They are also quite portable—you can take them anywhere with you. You can take them in cars, trains, and airplanes. You can take them to restaurants, friends' houses, and libraries. And you can—in fact it's the healthiest to do—take them out of doors all year long. If it's cold, bundle them up; if it's hot, make sure they're protected from the sun. Front carriers are excellent means of carrying an infant or young child; they permit you to go for long walks with your child, and despite their uncomfortable appearance, the reverse is true—infants love the snug support they receive, they love to be close to your body, and frequently they'll sleep for long periods as you walk through the woods, along a country road, or along city streets. Equally important, fathers love carrying their infants in front carriers because it gives them another opportunity to experience a special closeness with them.

Carriages are another excellent means of moving about with your infant. They're quite easy to move and they give your infant plenty of exposure to fresh air while he naps peacefully. Car seats are important; they give you a safe way of traveling with your infant for short or long distances. Some of the more substantial, untippable infant car seats can double as portable chairs for restaurants and other locations. Unfortunately, many people do not use car seats for infants.

Newborns can make great companions, and they benefit greatly by being with you. The more time they spend seeing you in different settings, the more they learn—the more colors and shapes and sounds and smells they become familiar with and the more people and places they see. John Cooney, a Parsippany, New Jersey, father, spent Saturdays working in his garage workshop with his infant son, Christopher. Secure in a comfortable, untiltable seat, Christopher delighted in watching his father work. Architect Henry Wollman often brings his one-month-old daughter Lilly to early morning business meetings. In short, you can take your newborn almost wherever and whenever you go. You then have more freedom and he is better for it. The most important thing, though, is that you or your wife are with him fairly frequently, so he has the security of your presence while a new world magically unfolds before him.

Finally, if you plan ahead regarding your child's birth, you'll be off to a good start. You'll have the time to spend with him and you'll use this time well in establishing a strong bond. You will no longer be a forgotten contributor to infant and child development. The more you are with your child, the closer you'll be to him. You'll be closer to your wife as well because you will have established a firm groundwork for a family in which both mother and father truly share in the exciting challenges of raising a child.

# Appendix

## CHAPTERS AND GROUPS OF THE AMERICAN SOCIETY FOR PSYCHOPROPHYLAXIS IN OBSTETRICS, INC.

Listed here are locations of ASPO chapters and groups. Since addresses change frequently, please contact ASPO Headquarters, 1411 K Street, N. W., Washington, DC 20005 for current addresses.

**ALABAMA**
ASPO of Central Alabama
Montgomery

**ARIZONA**
Arizona South Central ASPO
Scottsdale

**ARKANSAS**
PC, Inc.
Jacksonville

**CALIFORNIA**
ASPO of Los Angeles
San Pedro

Bay Area ASPO
Santa Clara

Birthing
Fairfield

CVPCEA
Stockton

Sacramento Valley ASPO
Sacramento

**COLORADO**
CPAC
Denver

Mile High ASPO
Aurora

**CONNECTICUT**
Connecticut CALM
Fairfield

**FLORIDA**
Jacksonville ASPO
Jacksonville

**GEORGIA**
ASPO for Greater Atlanta-Lamaze
Lilburn

**ILLINOIS**
ASPO of Central Illinois
Mt. Zion

ASPO of Northern Illinois
Mt. Prospect

**IOWA**
Siouxland CEA
Sioux City

**KANSAS**
CEA of Wichita
Wichita

**LOUISIANA**
ASPO on the Bayou
Crowley

**MARYLAND**
CAA
Cronsville

Delmarva ASPO
Mardela

DC Area ASPO
Adelphi

## MASSACHUSETTS
Lamaze Childbirth Education, Inc.
Watertown

PVCEA
Amherst

## MISSOURI
Gateway ASPO
Florissant

## NEW JERSEY
ASPO of Greater Camden
Clementon

ASPO of Northern New Jersey
Pompton Lake

ASPO of Princeton
Trenton

Central New Jersey ASPO
Oldbridge

Lamaze Childbirth Education of
  Hunterdon County
Frenchtown

Monmouth-Ocean ASPO
Hazlet

## NEW YORK
ASPO Long Island
Franklin Square

ASPO of New York City
Brooklyn

FMCA
Scotia

Long Island ASPO
Selden

Mid-Hudson ASPO
Wappingers Falls

Niagara Frontier ASPO
West Seneca

Westchester ASPO
White Plains

## NORTH CAROLINA
ASPO of Charlotte
Charlotte

Lamaze of Cary
Cary

Raleigh LIFE
Raleigh

## OREGON
LCL
Eugene

## PENNSYLVANIA
ASPO of Southeast Pennsylvania
Norristown

ASPO of Southwest Pennsylvania
Pittsburgh

Twin Tier ASPO
Mansfield

## SOUTH CAROLINA
ASPO of Greater Columbia
Columbia

## TENNESSEE
MCCE
Memphis

Nashville ASPO
Nashville

## TEXAS
ACTA
San Antonio

APEAL
Lubbock

DAPE
Mesquite

PEAEP
El Paso

San Angelo Childbirth Training
  Association
San Angelo

## VIRGINIA
ASPO of Tidewater
Virginia Beach

Charlotteville-Albemarle ASPO
Charlotteville

Peninsula ASPO
Newport News

Roanoke CEA
Vinton

Valley ASPO
Staunton

## WASHINGTON
PHP
Spokane

# CHAPTERS OF THE INTERNATIONAL CHILDBIRTH EDUCATION ASSOCIATION, INC.

## UNITED STATES

### ALABAMA
CEA of Greater Birmingham, Inc.
P. O. Box 3911
Birmingham, AL 35208

CEA of West Alabama
P. O. Box 3003
Tuscaloosa, AL 35404

Decatur CEA
P. O. Box 411
Decatur, AL 35602

Gulf Coast Area CEA
P. O. Box 6384
Mobile, AL 36606

### ALASKA
CEA of Greater Anchorage, Inc.
666 East 48th
Suite 214
Anchorage, AK 99502

North Star CEA
c/o Kathy Woller
SR Box 40446
Fairbanks, AK 99701

Parent and Child, Inc. of Juneau
535 Kennedy
Juneau, AK 99801

### ARIZONA
Arizona South Central Chapter of
ASPO
3010 West Morrow Drive
Phoenix, AZ 85027

### ARKANSAS
Arkansas Valley Parent Education
Association, Inc.
P. O. Box 1522
Russellville, AR 72801

Northwest Arkansas CEA
112 West Maple Street
Fayetteville, AR 72701

Prepared Childbirth, Inc.
P. O. Box 5821
Little Rock, AR 72215

### CALIFORNIA
Central Valley Prepared Childbirth
Educators Association
6434 Savannah
Stockton, CA 95209

CEA of Orange County
18142 Beneta Way
Tustin, CA 92680

CEA of San Diego, Inc.
3186 Adams Avenue
San Diego, CA 92116

CEA of Santa Cruz
1331 River Street
Santa Cruz, CA 95060

Childbirth Education League of the
Monterey Peninsula, Inc.
P. O. Box 6628
Carmel, CA 93921

Childbirth Education League of
Salinas
P. O. Box 1423
Salinas, CA 93901

Clovis Adult School Prepared
Childbirth Education
914 Fourth Street
Clovis, CA 93612

Read Natural Childbirth Foundation,
Inc.
1300 South Eliseo Drive
Suite 102
Greenbrae, CA 94904

Turlock CEA
2740 Andre Lane
Turlock, CA 95380

Yreka CEA
740 Meadowlark
Yreka, CA 96097

## COLORADO

Arkansas Valley CEA, Inc.
2011 Raton Avenue
La Junta, CO 81050

Association for Prepared Parenthood,
Inc.
P. O. Box 7292
Colorado Springs, CO 80933

Boulder County Lamaze
3622 Chase Court
Boulder, CO 80303

CEA of the Pikes Peak Region
P. O. Box 4641
Colorado Springs, CO 80930

Columbine Childbirth & Parenting
Education Association
c/o Kopf
941 County Road 129
Glenwood Springs, CO 81601

Mesa County CEA
P. O. Box 516
Grand Junction, CO 81501

Poudre Valley CEA, Inc.
P. O. Box 1433
Ft. Collins, CO 80522

San Luis Valley Preparation for
Childbirth
5293 South 4.7 Road
Alamosa, CO 81101

## CONNECTICUT

Babies
P. O. Box 377
Winsted, CT 06098

Calm Childbirth Association of the
Lamaze Method
c/o Disraelly
3 Nash Place
Stamford, CT 06906

Family Oriented Childbirth
Information Society, Inc.
P. O. Box 748
Manchester, CT 06040

Parenthood and Childbirth Education,
Inc.
1680 Albany Avenue
Hartford, CT 06105

## DELAWARE

Childbirth & Parenting Education
Associates, Inc.
P. O. Box 10541
Wilmington, DE 19850

Family Centered Parents, Inc.
P. O. Box 2653
Wilmington, DE 19850

## FLORIDA

CEA of Alachua County
1839 N.W. 31st Terrace
Gainesville, FL 32605

CEA of Broward County
3520 West Broward Boulevard
Suite 218 A
Ft. Lauderdale, FL 33312

CEA of Jacksonville
P. O. Box 8224
Jacksonville, FL 32211

CEA of Northwest Florida, Inc.
P. O. Box 1901
Pensacola, FL 32589

CEA of Okaloosa County
P. O. Box 709
Shalimar, FL 32579

CEA of Orange Park, Florida
P. O. Box 1101
Orange Park, FL 32073

CEA of the Palm Beaches, Inc.
1501 Whitehall Road
West Palm Beach, FL 33405

Childbirth & Parent Education
Association, Inc.
P. O. Box 264
South Miami, FL 33143

Childbirth & Parent Education
Association of Polk County
P. O. Box 655
Winter Haven, FL 33880

Childbirth & Parent Education League of
Pinellas County, Inc.
P. O. Box 1281
Largo, FL 33540

Parent & Childbirth Education
Association of Collier County, Inc.
34 10th Street, South
Naples, FL 33940

Parentcraft
P. O. Box 1535
Deland, FL 32720

Prepared Childbirth, Inc.
P. O. Box 2522
Daytona Beach, FL 32015

St. Anthony's CEA
601 12th Street, North
St. Petersburg, FL 33705

Sunshine CEA
7103 Pensacola Road
Fort Pierce, FL 33450

## GEORGIA
CEA of Augusta
P. O. Box 4091
Martinez, GA 30907

Childbirth & Parent Education
    Association
P. O. Box 696
Waycross, GA 31501

Griffin CEA
330 Anglin Road
Griffin, GA 30223

## HAWAII
Ahahui Kumu Hanau Association of
    Childbirth Educators
818 Keolu Drive
Kailu, HI 96734

Maui CEA
16 I Market Street
Wailuku, HI 96793

## IDAHO
Family Centered Education
    Association of Pocatello
P. O. Box 462
Pocatello, ID 83201

Prepared Childbirth Association
c/o Mrs. Caryl Hadley
Route 1
Sugar City, ID 83448

## ILLINOIS
Association for Childbirth Preparation
    & Family Life
P. O. Box 345
Macomb, IL 61455

CEA of Northwestern Illinois
1707 21st Street
Rock Island, IL 61201

Childbirth & Parent Education
    Association of Peoria
P. O. Box 24
Peoria, IL 61650

Midwest Parentcraft Center Auxiliary,
    Inc.
627 Beaver Road
Glenview, IL 60025

Parent & Childbirth Education Society
P. O. Box 213
Western Springs, IL 60558

Successful Childbirth & Organized
    Parent Education
P. O. Box 175
Crystal Lake, IL 60014

## INDIANA
Childbirth & Parenting, Inc.
P. O. Box 13
Richmond, IN 47374

Connersville CEA
Route 5, Box 88 A
Connersville, IN 47331

Lamaze Childbirth Education of
    Indianapolis
253 Restin Road
Greenwood, IN 46142

Maternity Family League
701 East 61st Street
Indianapolis, IN 46220

Parents & Friends of Children of
    Lincoln Hills, Inc.
P. O. Box 225
Corydon, IN 47112

Washington CEA
c/o Sara Hayden
Route 2, Cosby Road
Washington, IN 47501

## IOWA
CEA of Burlington
c/o Barb Miller
2648 Northwood
Burlington, IA 52601

CEA of Mississippi Valley, Inc.
P. O. Box 397
Bettendorf, IA 52722

CEA of Southeastern Iowa
P. O. Box 281
Fort Madison, IA 52627

CEA of Waterloo-Cedar Falls, Iowa
2413 Morrison Lane
Cedar Falls, IA 50612

Dubuque Childbirth & Parent
  Education Association
P. O. Box 54
Dubuque, IA 52001

Family Centered CEA
2531 West Euclid
Des Moines, IA 50310

Siouxland CEA
P. O. Box 531
Sioux City, IA 51102

## KANSAS
CEA of Greater Kansas City, Inc.
P. O. Box 1284
Mission, KS 66202

CEA of Wichita
345 North Hillside
Wichita, KS 67214

Childbirth & Parenting Education
  Association
P. O. Box 501
Leavenworth, KS 66048

Prepared Childbirth, Inc.
704 North 3rd Street
Lawrence, KS 66044

## KENTUCKY
Childbirth & Parenting Education
2732 Terrace Boulevard
Ashland, KY 41101

Christian County CEA
209 Hunting Creek Road
Hopkinsville, KY 42240

Families Together
152 Lorraine Court
Berea, KY 40403

Lexington Association for Parent
  Education
616 Montclair
Lexington, KY 40502

## LOUISIANA
Baton Rouge Parent-Child Association
11955 Sherbrook Drive
Baton Rouge, LA 70815

Lamaze Association for Childbirth
  Education
P. O. Box 1575
Morgan City, LA 70380

Northwest Louisiana CEA
3331 Youree Drive
Room L
Shreveport, LA 71105

Ouachita Parenting & Childbirth
  Association
P. O. Drawer 2174
West Monroe, LA 71291

Parenting & Childbirth Education
  Association of New Orleans
10120 Deerfield Drive
New Orleans, LA 70127

## MAINE
Hancock County Organization for
  Parenthood Education
c/o Audrey Carter
RFD 3
Surry, ME 04684

Maternal & Child Health Council, Inc.
46 Columbia Street
Bangor, ME 04401

Mid-Coast CEA
c/o Penny L. Bohac
RFD 1, Box 11-C
Brooks, ME 04921

Parent & Childbirth Education of
  Androscoggin Valley, Inc.
17 Warren Avenue
Lewiston, ME 04240

Parenthood Education Association
1 Summer Street
Hallowel, ME 04347

Waterville Area CEA
15 Summit Street
Fairfield, ME 04937

## MARYLAND
CEA of Baltimore, Inc.
11 West Pennsylvania
Suite 203
Towson, MD 21204

CEA of Greater Washington, DC, Inc.
P. O. Box 5078
Alexandria, VA 22305

Family Life & Maternity Education, Inc.
10113 Parkwood Terrace
Bethesda, MD 20014

## MASSACHUSETTS
Berkshire-Bennington Parent
  Education Association
11 Greene Avenue
North Adams, MA 01247

Boston Association for Childbirth
  Education
P. O. Box 29
Newtonville, MA 02160

CEA of Central Massachusetts, Inc.
Box 193
West Side Station
Worcester, MA 01602

CEA of Greater Fall River
136 Statle Avenue
Somerset, MA 02726

COPE (Coping with the Overall
  Pregnancy/Parenting Experience)
37 Clarendon Street
Boston, MA 02116

Pioneer Valley CEA, Inc.
P. O. Box 699
Amherst, MA 01002

## MICHIGAN
Association for Prepared Childbirth
1101 Watson Road
Mt. Pleasant, MI 48858

Association for Shared Childbirth, Inc.
1514 West Saginaw
Lansing, MI 48195

Big Rapids Association for Prepared
  Childbirth
Box 136, Route 2
Big Rapids, MI 49307

Cadillac Childbirth Association, Inc.
P. O. Box 165
Cadillac, MI 49601

CEA of Manistee
P. O. Box 72
Manistee, MI 49660

CEA of Marquette County
1305 Northrop
Marquette, MI 49855

Childbirth Information Service, Inc.
P. O. Box 36451
Grosse Pointe, MI 48236

Childbirth Preparation Association
P. O. Box 73
Lincoln Park, MI 48146

Childbirth Preparation Service of
  Jackson, Inc.
P. O. Box 742
Jackson, MI 49204

Dickinson County CEA
915 East Main
Iron Mountain, MI 49801

Family Life Forum, Inc.
P. O. Box 7193
Ann Arbor, MI 48107

Joys of Parenthood
Route 5, Box 149 A
Dowagiac, MI 49047

Kalamazoo Association for Prepared
  Childbirth
P. O. Box 364
Richland, MI 49083

Lamaze Childbirth Association of
  Greater Detroit, Inc.
c/o Jo Lynn Watts
2075 Bacon
Berkley, MI 48072

Lamaze Childbirth Education, Inc. of
  Grand Rapids
P. O. Box 284
Jenison, MI 49428

Lamaze CEA of Livonia, Inc.
P. O. Box 2811
Livonia, MI 48151

Lamaze Childbirth Preparation
  Association of Ann Arbor, Inc.
P. O. Box 1812
Ann Arbor, MI 48106

Lenawee County Prepared
  Childbirth Service
P. O. Box 632
Adrian, MI 49221

Parent Education Program
c/o Dee Stafford
401 Nebobish
Essexville, MI 48732

Parents Inc. of Albion
P. O. Box 584
Albion, MI 49224

Plymouth CEA
28425 Peppermill Road
Farmington Hills, MI 48018

Saginaw Valley CEA
P. O. Box 657
Bay City, MI 48707

Wurtsmith CEA
5356 Hughes Street
Oscoda, MI 48750

## MINNESOTA
Austin CEA
Route 1, Box 202 A
Lyle, MN 55953

CEA of Fairmont
1417 North Park Street
Fairmont, MN 56031

CEA of Greater Minneapolis/St. Paul,
  Inc.
2101 Hennepin Avenue
Minneapolis, MN 55405

CEA of Kanabec County
715 Riverside
Mora, MN 55051

CEA of Renville County
c/o Mary Ryan
RR 1, Box 278
Bird Island, MN 55310

CEA of St. Cloud
P. O. Box 483
St. Cloud, MN 56301

CEA of Southeastern Minnesota, Inc.
P. O. Box 6522
Rochester, MN 55901

CEA of Southwest Minnesota
112 North Sverdrup
Jackson, MN 56143

CEA of Two Harbors
P. O. Box 291
Two Harbors, MN 55616

Faribault Area CEA
P. O. Box 253
Fairbault, MN 55021

Mesabi CEA
c/o Judy Zehren
RR 1, Box 173 C
Britt, MN 55710

Northfield CEA, Inc.
P. O. Box 233
Northfield, MN 55057

Park Rapids Childbirth Education
  Classes
Hubbard County Nursing Service
Courthouse
Park Rapids, MN 56470

Scott-Carver CEA
132 Rustle Road
Jordan, MN 55318

Shared Childbirth Association of
  Mankato
c/o Rosy Carlstrom
Route 1, Box 224 C
Mankato, MN 56001

## MISSISSIPPI
Coast Association for Parent
  Education, Inc.
P. O. Box 389
Ocean Springs, MS 39564

## MISSOURI
CEA of Greater Kansas City, Inc.
P. O. Box 1284
Mission, KS 66202

Childbirth & Parent Education, Inc., of
  Kansas City
P. O. Box 17725
Kansas City, MO 64134

Childbirth Preparation Classes of
  Cape Girardeau
P. O. Box 1164
Cape Girardeau, MO 63701

Childbirth Preparation Seminar of
  Greater Kansas City, Inc.
1600 Country Club Drive
Pleasant Hill, MO 64080

Childbirth Without Pain Education
  League, Inc., Springfield Chapter
2430 Manchester
Springfield, MO 65804

Childbirth With Preparation of
  Johnson County
505 East North
Warrensburg, MO 64093

Expectant Parents Class
Children's Therapy Center
600 East 14th Street
Sedalia, MO 65301

Parent & Child/St. Louis
P. O. Box 9985
Kirkwood, MO 63122

## NEBRASKA
CEA Mid-Plains, North Platte
2815 Cedarberry Lane
North Platte, NB 69101

CEA of Western Nebraska, Inc.
P. O. Box 937
Scottsbluff, NB 69361

Childbirth & Parent Education
Association of Lincoln, Inc.
P. O. Box 6402
Lincoln, NB 68506

## NEW HAMPSHIRE
Family Health Programs, Inc.
Globe Shopping Center
Gorham, NH 03581

La Famille, Inc.
c/o Judie Spaulding
16 West Park Street
Claremont, NH 03743

## NEW JERSEY
Cape/Atlantic CEA
P. O. Box 156
Linwood, NJ 08221

CEA of South Jersey, Inc.
P. O. Box 462
Toms River, NJ 08753

Childbirth & Parent Education
Association
P. O. Box 163
Cape May, NJ 08210

Childbirth & Parent Education
Association of Northern New Jersey
P. O. Box 381
Dover, NJ 07801

Northern New Jersey Chapter of
ASPO
P. O. Box 562
Ridgewood, NJ 07540

## NEW MEXICO
Albuquerque CEA
P. O. Box 26173
Albuquerque, NM 87125

Farmington Association for Childbirth
Education
P. O. Box 2911
Farmington, NM 87401

Lamaze Childbirth Education
P. O. Box 422
LaLuz, NM 88337

Santa Fe CEA, Inc.
1702 Callejon Cordelia
Santa Fe, NM 87501

## NEW YORK
The Arnot-Ogden Family Craft Group
Arnot-Ogden Memorial Hospital
Elmira, NY 14901

CEA of Albany, N.Y.
P. O. Box 3
Albany, NY 12201

CEA of Cayuga County
P. O. Box 444
Auburn, NY 13021

CEA of Greater Syracuse, Inc.
P. O. Box 15
Syracuse, NY 13201

CEA of Rochester, Inc.
1921 Norton Street
Rochester, NY 14609

CEA of Tompkins County
15 Lake Street
Dryden, NY 13053

Metropolitan New York CEA
30 Beekman Place
New York, NY 10022

Oswego County CEA
234 East 7th Street
Oswego, NY 13126

Project: Child Growth
P. O. Box 787
Glen Cove, NY 11542

Westchester-Putnam CEA
P. O. Box 112
Croton-on-Hudson, NY 10520

## NORTH CAROLINA

Eastern Regional Childbirth Educators
  of North Carolina
126 Fox Drive
Dudley, NC 28333

## OHIO

Cace/Lamaze
P. O. Box 2545
Columbus, OH 43216

Canton CEA
1225 North Main Street, Box G
North Canton, OH 44720

Center for Humane Options in the
  Childbirth Experience
Woodward Park Medical Center
1300 Morse Road
Columbus, OH 43229

Childbirth Education Association
P. O. Box 5051
Cincinnati, OH 45205

CEA of Akron
P. O. Box 1061
Akron, OH 44309

CEA of Cleveland, Inc.
P. O. Box 21271
Cleveland, OH 44121

Childbirth & Parent Education, Inc.
4011 Hillman Way
Youngstown, OH 44512

Childbirth & Parenting Education
  Association
P. O. Box 283
Kent, OH 44240

Cloverleaf Organization for Parent
  Education
P. O. Box 852
Cambridge, OH 43725

Educated Childbirth, Inc.
P. O. Box 2613
Lakewood, OH 44107

Family-Centered Association for
  Childbirth Education, Inc.
P. O. Box 2826
Mansfield, OH 44906

Firelands CEA
1913 Cleveland Road, West
Huron, OH 44839

Fremont CEA, Inc.
1811 Ernest Drive
Fremont, OH 43420

Lamaze Childbirth Association-
  Parents
2137 Belcher Drive
Columbus, OH 43224

Parents' Association for Childbirth
  Education
P. O. Box 70
Marion, OH 43302

Parents Educating Parents
c/o 480 Courtney
Newark, OH 43055

Parents for Prepared Childbirth, Inc.
P. O. Box 591
Marietta, OH 45750

Prepared Childbirth, Inc.
P. O. Box 591
Elyria, OH 44035

Salem Childbirth, Inc.
P. O. Box 4117
Salem, OH 44460

Tiffin CEA
P. O. Box 673
Tiffin, OH 44883

Total Parent Education of Greater
  Cincinnati, Inc.
P. O. Box 2921
Cincinnati, OH 45201

The Trained Childbirth Association of
  Lancaster & Fairfield County
P. O. Box 1033
Lancaster, OH 43130

Tri-County Trained Childbirth
  Association
1789 Newlove Road
South Charleston, OH 45368

Warren CEA
1119 Prince Drive
Cortland, OH 44410

Wayne County CEA
P. O. Box 568
Wooster, OH 44691

## OKLAHOMA

Central Oklahoma CEA
P. O. Box 25606
Oklahoma City, OK 73125

CEA of Tulsa, Inc.
Route 1, Box 583
Sapulpa, OK 74066

Childbirth & Family Life, Inc.
P. O. Box 52422
Tulsa, OK 74152

Childbirth Preparation League
1220 South Johnstone
Bartlesville, OK 74003

## OREGON
Central Oregon Childbirth Educators
220 N.W. Oregon Avenue
Bend, OR 97701

CEA of Southern Oregon
P. O. Box 1394
Medford, OR 97501

Lamaze (ASPO) Teachers of Roseburg
627 N.E. Madrona
Myrtle Creek, OR 97426

Prepared Childbirth Association
6446 S.W. Capitol Highway
Portland, OR 97201

## PENNSYLVANIA
Berks County Association for
    Childbirth Education
P. O. Box 6139
Reading, PA 19610

CEA of Beaver County
115 North Mercer Avenue
New Brighton, PA 15066

CEA of Erie
P. O. Box 824
Erie, PA 16512

CEA of the Greater Monongahela
    Valley
173 Victoria Drive
Monongahela, PA 15063

CEA of Greater Philadelphia
814 Fayette Street
Conshohocken, PA 19428

CEA of Greater Washington Area
c/o Sherry Lane
R.D. 1, Box 30
Canonsburg, PA 15317

CEA of Luzerne County
19 Valley View Drive
Swoyersville, PA 18704

CEA of Northeastern Pennsylvania,
    Inc.
P. O. Box 814
Scranton, PA 18501

CEA of the Poconos
P. O. Box 641
Stroudsburg, PA 18360

CEA, Inc. of State College
P. O. Box 1074
State College, PA 16801

Clarion Organization for Parent
    Education
c/o Ping Lillstrom
Windhound Farm
New Bethlehem, PA 16242

Clearfield Area Prepared Childbirth
    Association
216 South Front Street
Clearfield, PA 16830

Dubois Area Prepared Childbirth
    Association
P. O. Box 35
Brockway, PA 15824

F.A.M.L.E.E.
P. O. Box 15
Telford, PA 18969

Grove City Area CEA
RD 1, Box 96
West Sunbury, PA 16061

Lebanon Valley CEA, Inc.
RD 7, Box 235
Lebanon, PA 17042

Parents' Association for Childbirth
    Education
P. O. Box 14429
Philadelphia, PA 19115

Pittsburgh Organization for Childbirth
    Education, Inc.
P. O. Box 10647
Pittsburgh, PA 15235

Prepared Childbirth Education
P. O. Box 2771
Lehigh Valley, PA 18001

Wayne County CEA
355 Ridge Street
Honesdale, PA 18431

## SOUTH DAKOTA

Lewis & Clark CEA
c/o USD School of Medicine
1017 West 5th
Yankton, SD 57078

Sioux Falls Educated Childbirth
  Association
P. O. Box 34
Sioux Falls, SD 57101

## TENNESSEE

CEA of Oak Ridge, Tennessee, Inc.
P. O. Box 551
Oak Ridge, TN 37830

Organization for the Art of
  Parenthood
330 Peterson Lane
Clarksville, TN 37040

## TEXAS

Arlington Organization for Parent
  Education
P. O. Box 1261
Arlington, TX 76010

CEA of Galveston, Texas
101 Albacore
Galveston, TX 77550

CEA of Victoria
P. O. Box 3852
Victoria, TX 77901

Childbirth & Parent Education Society
P. O. Box 1585
Sherman, TX 75090

Childbirth With Preparation
c/o Renee Hillis
Route 11, Box 149–B3
Lubbock, TX 79407

Corpus Christi Organization for Parent
  Education
325 Williamson Place
Corpus Christi, TX 78411

Nacogdoches Parents Association
524 Bremond
Nacogdoches, TX 75961

Southeast Association for Childbirth
  Education, Inc.
P. O. Box 57124
Webster, TX 77598

## UTAH

Cache Valley CEA
P. O. Box 581
Logan, UT 84321

## VIRGINIA

CEA of Greater Washington, DC, Inc.
P. O. Box 5078
Alexandria, VA 22305

CEA of the New River Valley
P. O. Box 801
Blacksburg, VA 24060

Child and Parent
1413 Winchester Street
Fredericksburg, VA 22401

Parent Education League of Lynchburg
P. O. Box 2332
Lynchburg, VA 24501

Prepared Childbirth Association of
  Tidewater, Inc.
601 West Kingston Lane
Virginia Beach, VA 23452

Roanoke Childbirth Educators &
  Associates
Roanoke Memorial Hospital
Box D
Roanoke, VA 24033

## WASHINGTON

CEA of Coulee Dam
General Delivery
Coulee Dam, WA 99116

CEA of Seattle
1433 NW 54th Street
Seattle, WA 98107

CEA of Tacoma
31116 48th Avenue, East
Graham, WA 98338

Childbirth & Parent Education
  Association of the Tri-Cities, Inc.
P. O. Box 6222
Kennewick, WA 99336

Clark County CEA
P. O. Box 2531
Vancouver, WA 98661

Mid-Columbia Childhood Education
  Association
P. O. Box 897
White Salmon, WA 98672

Parent Association for Learning
P. O. Box 767
Aberdeen, WA 98520

Preparation for Expectant Parents
P. O. Box 33532
Seattle, WA 98133

Prepared Childbirth Association in
　Bellingham
P. O. Box 1407
Bellingham, WA 98225

Spokane's Association for Family
　Education
P. O. Box 9016
Spokane, WA 99209

Whidbey CEA
7493 750th Avenue
Oak Harbor, WA 98277

## WEST VIRGINIA

CEA of Fairmont
P. O. Box 263
Fairmont, WV 26554

CEA of the Greater Kanawha Valley,
　Inc.
P. O. Box 939
St. Albans, WV 25177

CEA of Huntington, Inc.
2105 Inwood Drive
Huntington, WV 25701

CEA of the Mid-Ohio Valley
P. O. Box 856
Parkersburg, WV 26101

Parent & Childbirth Education
　Association
6 Hospital Plaza
Clarksburg, WV 26301

Prepared Childbirth of Beckley, Inc.
106 Murray Street
Beckley, WV 25801

## WISCONSIN

Childbirth Association Lamaze
　Method of Janesville
P. O. Box 1041
Janesville, WI 53545

CEA of Green Bay, Inc.
P. O. Box 54
Green Bay, WI 54305

CEA of Milwaukee, Inc.
5636 West Burleigh
Milwaukee, WI 53210

CEA of St. Croix Valley
P. O. Box 345
Hudson, WI 54016

Childbirth Education Services of
　Racine
P. O. Box 714
Racine, WI 53401

Childbirth & Parent Education
　Association of Madison, Inc.
P. O. Box 565
Madison, WI 53701

Educated Childbirth Association of
　Waukesha County
426 Lemira Avenue
Waukesha, WI 53186

Hayward Area CEA
127 North First Street
Hayward, WI 54843

Marinette-Menominee CEA
P. O. Box 393
Marinette, WI 54143

Northland CEA, Inc.
124 Baird
Rhinelander, WI 54501

Sheboygan CEA
818 Swift Avenue
Sheboygan, WI 53081

Stevens Point Area CEA
2522n North Reserve Drive
Stevens Point, WI 54481

## WYOMING

Casper Family Centered League
c/o 2934 Belmont Road
Casper, WY 82601

Cheyenne CEA
112 West First Avenue
Cheyenne, WY 82001

Parent & Childbirth Association of
　Laramie
c/o Judy Olson
2118 Thornburgh
Laramie, WY 82070

# CANADA

## ALBERTA
Edmonton CEA
c/o Diane Martz
304 Southbridge
(106th & 45th Avenues)
Edmonton, Alberta T6H 4M9

Foothill's Hospital Prenatal
  Instructions
9120 48th Avenue, NW
Calgary, Alberta T3B 2B2

Grande Prairie CEA
Postal Box 1287
Grande Prairie, Alberta T8V 4Z1

## BRITISH COLUMBIA
Childbirth With Confidence
22820 Westminster Highway
Richmond, British Columbia V6V 1B7

Lower Mainland Childbearing Society
3545 West 43rd Avenue
Vancouver, British Columbia V6N 3J8

Mission CEA
c/o Iris Todd
RR 2
8730 McLean Street
Mission, British Columbia V2V 4H9

Vancouver Childbirth Association
256–4664 Lougheed Highway
Burnaby, British Columbia V5C 5T5

Victoria Lamaze CEA
301 Moss Street
Victoria, British Columbia V8V 4M7

## MANITOBA
Winnipeg CEA
926 Oakenwald Avenue
Winnipeg, Manitoba R3T 1N3

## NEW BRUNSWICK
Fredericton CEA
c/o Deb Staples
166 McKeen Street
Fredericton, New Brunswick E3A 2R1

## NEWFOUNDLAND
St. John's Childbirth & Parent
  Education Association
8 Ordance Street
St. John's, Newfoundland A1C 3K7

## ONTARIO
CEA of Toronto
33 Price Street
Toronto, Ontario M4W 1Z2

CEA of Windsor
P. O. Box 7224
Windsor, Ontario N9C 3Z1

Educated Childbirth Organization
12329 Riverside Drive
Tecumseh, Ontario N8N 1A4

Kingston CEA, Inc.
251 Willingdon Avenue
Kingston, Ontario K7L 4J2

Lamaze Prepared Childbirth Group
c/o 99 Brock Street
Timmins, Ontario P4N 7N9

London CEA
699 Fanshawe Park Road
London, Ontario N5X 1L4

Ottawa-Hull CEA
P. O. Box 4142
Station E
Ottawa, Ontario K1S 5B2

Sarnia CEA
132 Cedar Crescent
Sarnia, Ontario N7T 4J5

## SASKATCHEWAN
Regina CEA
3175 Angus Street
Regina, Saskatchewan S4S 1P5

Saskatoon CEA
c/o 608 Walmer Road
Saskatoon, Saskatchewan S7L 0E2

# THE PREGNANT PATIENT'S BILL OF RIGHTS

# THE PREGNANT PATIENT'S RESPONSIBILITIES

The International Childbirth Education Association (ICEA) is an interdisciplinary, volunteer organization representing groups and individuals who share a genuine interest in the goals of family-centered maternity care and education for the childbearing year.

ICEA constantly seeks to expand awareness of the rights and responsibilities of pregnant women and expectant parents. Most pregnant women are not aware of their rights or of the obstetrician's legal obligation to obtain their informed consent to treatment. The American College of Obstetricians and Gynecologists has made a commendable effort to clearly set forth the pregnant patient's right of informed consent in the following excerpts from pages 66 and 67 of its *Standards for Obstetric-Gynecologic Services.*

"It is important to note the distinction between 'consent' and 'informed consent'. Many physicians, because they do not realize there is a difference, believe they are free from liability if the patient consents to treatment. This is not true. The physician may still be liable if the patient's consent was not informed. In addition, the usual consent obtained by a hospital does not in any way release the physician from his legal duty of obtaining an informed consent from his patient.

*"Most courts consider that the patient is 'informed' if the following information is given:*

• The processes contemplated by the physician as treatment, including whether the treatment is new or unusual.
• The risks and hazards of the treatment.
• The chances for recovery after treatment.
• The necessity of the treatment.
• The feasibility of alternative methods of treatment."

"One point on which courts do agree is that explanations must be given in such a way that the patient understands them. A physician cannot claim as a defense that he explained the procedure to the patient when he knew the patient did not understand. The physician has a duty to act with due care under the circumstances; this means he must be sure the patient understands what she is told."

"It should be emphasized that the following reasons are not sufficient to justify failure to inform:

1. That the patient may prefer not to be told the unpleasant possibilities regarding the treatment.
2. That full disclosure might suggest infinite dangers to a patient with an active imagination, thereby causing her to refuse treatment.
3. That the patient, on learning the risks involved, might rationally decline treatment. The right to decline is the specific fundamental right protected by the informed consent doctrine."

*On the following pages ICEA sets forth the **Pregnant Patient's Bill of Rights** along with the **Pregnant Patient's Responsibilities.***

# THE PREGNANT PATIENT'S BILL OF RIGHTS

American parents are becoming increasingly aware that well-intentioned health professionals do not always have scientific data to support common American obstetrical practices and that many of these practices are carried out primarily because they are part of medical and hospital tradition. In the last forty years many artificial practices have been introduced which have changed childbirth from a physiological event to a very complicated medical procedure in which all kinds of drugs are used and procedures carried out, sometimes unnecessarily, and many of them potentially damaging for the baby and even for the mother. A growing body of research makes it alarmingly clear that every aspect of traditional American hospital care during labor and delivery must now be questioned as to its possible effect on the future well-being of both the obstetric patient and her unborn child.

One in every 35 children born in the United States today will eventually be diagnosed as retarded; in 75% of these cases there is no familial or genetic predisposing factor. One in every 10 to 17 children has been found to have some form of brain dysfunction or learning disability requiring special treatment. Such statistics are not confined to the lower socioeconomic group but cut across all segments of American society.

New concerns are being raised by childbearing women because no one knows what degree of oxygen depletion, head compression, or traction by forceps the unborn or newborn infant can tolerate before that child sustains permanent brain damage or dysfunction. The recent findings regarding the cancer-related drug diethylstilbestrol have alerted the public to the fact that neither the approval of a drug by the U.S. Food and Drug Administration nor the fact that a drug is prescribed by a physician serves as a guarantee that a drug or medication is safe for the mother or her unborn child. In fact, the American Academy of Pediatrics' Committee on Drugs has recently stated that there is no drug, whether prescription or over-the-counter remedy, which has been proven safe for the unborn child.

The Pregnant Patient has the right to participate in decisions involving her well-being and that of her unborn child, unless there is a clearcut medical emergency that prevents her participation. In addition to the rights set forth in the American Hospital Association's "Patient's Bill of Rights," (which has also been adopted by the New York City Department of Health) the Pregnant Patient, because she represents TWO patients rather than one, should be recognized as having the additional rights listed below.

1. *The Pregnant Patient has the right, prior to the administration of any drug or procedure, to be informed by the health professional caring for her of any potential direct or indirect effects, risks or hazards to herself or her unborn or newborn infant which may result from the use of a drug or procedure prescribed for or administered to her during pregnancy, labor, birth or lactation.*

2. *The Pregnant Patient has the right, prior to the proposed therapy, to be informed, not only of the benefits, risks and hazards of the proposed therapy but also of known alternative therapy, such as available childbirth education classes which could help to prepare the Pregnant Patient physically and mentally to cope with the discomfort or stress of pregnancy and the experience of childbirth, thereby reducing or eliminating her need for drugs and obstetric intervention. She should be offered such information early in her pregnancy in order that she may make a reasoned decision.*

3. *The Pregnant Patient has the right, prior to the administration of any drug, to be informed by the health professional who is prescribing or administering the drug to her that any drug which she receives during pregnancy, labor and birth, no matter how or when the drug is taken or administered, may adversely affect her unborn baby, directly or indirectly, and that there is no drug or chemical which has been proven safe for the unborn child.*

4. *The Pregnant Patient has the right if Cesarean birth is anticipated, to be informed prior to the administration of any drug, and preferably prior to her hospitalization, that minimizing her and, in turn, her baby's intake of nonessential pre-operative medicine will benefit her baby.*

5. *The Pregnant Patient has the right, prior to the administration of a drug or procedure, to be informed of the areas of uncertainty if there is NO properly controlled follow-up re-*

search which has established the safety of the drug or procedure with regard to its direct and/or indirect effects on the physiological, mental and neurological development of the child exposed, via the mother, to the drug or procedure during pregnancy, labor, birth or lactation—(this would apply to virtually all drugs and the vast majority of obstetric procedures).

6. The Pregnant Patient has the right, prior to the administration of any drug, to be informed of the brand name and generic name of the drug in order that she may advise the health professional of any past adverse reaction to the drug.

7. The Pregnant Patient has the right to determine for herself, without pressure from her attendant, whether she will accept the risks inherent in the proposed therapy or refuse a drug or procedure.

8. The Pregnant Patient has the right to know the name and qualifications of the individual administering a medication or procedure to her during labor or birth.

9. The Pregnant Patient has the right to be informed, prior to the administration of any procedure, whether that procedure is being administered to her for her or her baby's benefit (medically indicated) or as an elective procedure (for convenience, teaching purposes or research).

10. The Pregnant Patient has the right to be accompanied during the stress of labor and birth by someone she cares for, and to whom she looks for emotional comfort and encouragement.

11. The Pregnant Patient has the right after appropriate medical consultation to choose a position for labor and for birth which is least stressful to her baby and to herself.

12. The Obstetric Patient has the right to have her baby cared for at her bedside if her baby is normal, and to feed her baby according to her baby's needs rather than according to the hospital regimen.

13. The Obstetric Patient has the right to be informed in writing of the name of the person who actually delivered her baby and the professional qualifications of that person. This information should also be on the birth certificate.

14. The Obstetric Patient has the right to be informed if there is any known or indicated aspect of her or her baby's care or condition which may cause her or her baby later difficulty or problems.

15. The Obstetric Patient has the right to have her and her baby's hospital medical records complete, accurate and legible and to have their records, including Nurses' Notes, retained by the hospital until the child reaches at least the age of majority, or, alternatively, to have the records offered to her before they are destroyed.

16. The Obstetric Patient, both during and after her hospital stay, has the right to have access to her complete hospital medical records, including Nurses' Notes, and to receive a copy upon payment of a reasonable fee and without incurring the expense of retaining an attorney.

It is the obstetric patient and her baby, not the health professional, who must sustain any trauma or injury resulting from the use of a drug or obstetric procedure. The observation of the rights listed above will not only permit the obstetric patient to participate in the decisions involving her and her baby's health care, but will help to protect the health professional and the hospital against litigation arising from resentment or misunderstanding on the part of the mother.

**Prepared by Doris Haire, Chair., ICEA Committee on Health Law and Regulation**

# THE PREGNANT PATIENT'S RESPONSIBILITIES

*In addition to understanding her rights the Pregnant Patient should also understand that she too has certain responsibilities. The Pregnant Patient's responsibilities include the following:*

1. The Pregnant Patient is responsible for learning about the physical and psychological process of labor, birth and postpartum recovery. The better informed expectant parents are the better they will be able to participate in decisions concerning the planning of their care.
2. The Pregnant Patient is responsible for learning what comprises good prenatal and intranatal care and for making an effort to obtain the best care possible.
3. Expectant parents are responsible for knowing about those hospital policies and regulations which will affect their birth and postpartum experience.
4. The Pregnant Patient is responsible for arranging for a companion or support person (husband, mother, sister, friend, etc.) who will share in her plans for birth and who will accompany her during her labor and birth experience.
5. The Pregnant Patient is responsible for making her preferences known clearly to the health professionals involved in her case in a courteous and cooperative manner and for making mutually agreed-upon arrangements regarding maternity care alternatives with her physician and hospital in advance of labor.
6. Expectant parents are responsible for listening to their chosen physician or midwife with an open mind, just as they expect him or her to listen openly to them.
7. Once they have agreed to a course of health care, expectant parents are responsible, to the best of their ability, for seeing that the program is carried out in consultation with others with whom they have made the agreement.
8. The Pregnant Patient is responsible for obtaining information in advance regarding the approximate cost of her obstetric and hospital care.
9. The Pregnant Patient who intends to change her physician or hospital is responsible for notifying all concerned, well in advance of the birth if possible, and for informing both of her reasons for changing.
10. In all their interactions with medical and nursing personnel, the expectant parents should behave towards those caring for them with the same respect and consideration they themselves would like.
11. During the mother's hospital stay the mother is responsible for learning about her and her baby's continuing care after discharge from the hospital.
12. After birth, the parents should put into writing constructive comments and feelings of satisfaction and/or dissatisfaction with the care (nursing, medical and personal) they received. Good service to families in the future will be facilitated by those parents who take the time and responsibility to write letters expressing their feelings about the maternity care they received.

All the previous statements assume a normal birth and postpartum experience. Expectant parents should realize that, if complications develop in their cases, there will be an increased need to trust the expertise of the physician and hospital staff they have chosen. However, if problems occur, the childbearing woman still retains her responsibility for making informed decisions about her care or treatment and that of her baby. If she is incapable of assuming that responsibility because of her physical condition, her previously authorized companion or support person should assume responsibility for making informed decisions on her behalf.

**Prepared by Members of ICEA**

*For a complimentary copy send a stamped, self-addressed envelope to*
*Box 1900, New York, NY 10001*
*Bulk orders available from ICEA Publication/Distribution Center,*
*P.O. Box 3825, Brighton Station, Rochester, NY 14610*

# Bibliography

**Chapter 1**

Whalen, Elizabeth. *A Baby . . . Maybe.* New York: Bobbs-Merrill, 1976.

**Chapter 2**

Biller, Henry and Dennis Meredith. *Father Power.* New York: Doubleday (Anchor), 1975.

Green, Maureen. *Fathering: A New Look at the Creative Art of Being a Father.* New York: McGraw-Hill, 1977.

**Chapter 3**

Colman, Arthur and Libby. *Pregnancy: The Psychological Experience.* New York: Bantam, 1971.

Guttmacher, Alan F. *Pregnancy, Birth, and Family Planning.* New York: Signet, 1973.

Montagu, Ashley. *Life Before Birth.* New York: New American Library, 1964.

Rugh, Roberts and Landrum B. Shettles. *From Conception to Birth: The Drama of Life's Beginnings.* New York: Harper & Row, 1971.

**Chapter 4**

Bing, Elisabeth and Libby Colman. *Making Love During Pregnancy.* New York: Bantam, 1977.

**Chapter 5**

Porter, Sylvia. *Sylvia Porter's New Money Book.* New York: Doubleday, 1979.

**Chapter 6**

Bing, Elisabeth. *Six Practical Lessons for an Easier Childbirth.* New York: Bantam, 1977.

Bing, Elisabeth and Libby Colman. *Having a Baby after Thirty.* New York: Bantam, 1980.

Bradley, Robert A. *Husband-Coached Childbirth.* New York: Harper & Row, 1974.

Brewer, Gail S. *The Pregnancy after 30 Workbook: A Program for Safe Childbearing—No Matter What Your Age.* Emmaus, Pa.: Rodale Press, 1978.

Dick-Read, Grantly. *Childbirth without Fear.* New York: Harper & Row, 1970.

Karmel, Marjorie. *Thank You, Dr. Lamaze.* New York: Doubleday, 1959.

Walton, Vicki. *Have It Your Way.* New York: Bantam, 1978.

**Chapter 7**

Kitzinger, Sheila. *The Experience of Childbirth.* New York: Penguin, 1978.

Klaus, Marshall and John Kennel. *Maternal and Infant Bonding: The Impact of Early Separation or Loss on Family Development.* St. Louis, Mo.: C. V. Mosby, 1976.

**Chapter 8**
Brazelton, T. Berry. *Infants and Mothers.* New York: Delta, 1970.
Fraiberg, Selma. *The Magic Years.* New York: Scribner, 1959.
Levine, James E. *Who Will Raise the Children? New Options for Fathers (and Mothers).* New York: Bantam, 1977.
Rakowitz, Elly and Gloria S. Rubin. *Living with Your New Baby: A Postpartum Guide for Mothers and Fathers.* New York: Berkeley Publishing, 1979.

# Index